STEP ZERO

About the authors:
Arnold M. Washton, Ph.D., a licensed psychologist, is founding director of The Washton Institute, an outpatient alcoholism and substance abuse treatment center in New York City. An internationally recognized clinician, researcher, and public speaker, he has appeared frequently in the national media and is the author of numerous books and articles on the treatment of addiction, including: *The Cocaine Recovery Workbooks* (Hazelden Educational Materials, 1990); *Cocaine Addiction: Treatment, Recovery, and Relapse Prevention* (Norton, 1989); and with Donna Boundy, *Willpower's Not Enough: Understanding and Recovering from Addictions of Every Kind* (HarperCollins, 1990).

Nannette Stone-Washton, M.S., assistant director of The Washton Institute, is a nationally known specialist in treating women and couples affected by chemical dependency. She has produced a variety of educational materials about recovery and is coauthor of *Cocaine: Seduction and Solution* (Clarkson N. Potter, 1984).

STEP ZERO

Getting to Recovery

Arnold M. Washton, Ph.D.
Nannette Stone-Washton, M.S.

 HAZELDEN®

First published October 1991.

Copyright © 1991, Hazelden Foundation.
All rights reserved. No portion of this publication
may be reproduced in any manner without the written
permission of the publisher.

ISBN: 0-89486-785-7

Library of Congress Catalog Card Number: 91-72176

Printed in the United States of America.

Editor's note:
Hazelden Educational Materials offers a variety of informa-
tion on chemical dependency and related areas. Our publica-
tions do not necessarily represent Hazelden's programs, nor do
they officially speak for any Twelve Step organization.

To our daughters, Tala and Danae, and their grandparents, Edward and Nadine Smart, who help us keep things in perspective.

Contents

Acknowledgments

We offer heartfelt thanks to the people who helped us with this book. Sid Farrar and Bill Chickering of Hazelden Educational Materials supported this project from its inception. Guy Kettelhack, an extraordinarily gifted writer, editor, and thinker sculpted into words our ideas about Step Zero and added more than a few good ideas of his own. We could not have done this project without him. Our patients supplied the raw material for this book and we thank them for the opportunity to be part of their lives. Our sincere thanks to members of our clinical staff, especially Andrew Tatarsky, Ph.D.; Edward J. Poska, CAC; Robin Lightman, CSW, CAC; and Margo Harrison, CSW, who have helped us put the concept of Step Zero into clinical practice.

Note to Readers

While all of the stories in *Step Zero* are based on the real experience of recovering people, identifying details have been completely altered to preserve anonymity.

We would also like to suggest that any important decisions about your health or what to do about recovery be made in concert with a therapist or treatment professional. This book is not offered as a substitute for treatment or professional advice.

CHAPTER ONE

A New Look At Where You Are Now

You've just opened a book—*yet another book about addiction,* you may be saying to yourself. If you're like many of the thousands of people we've worked with as therapists dealing with substance abuse and compulsive behavior, you have a number of expectations. *They're going to show me how to tell if I'm an addict,* you may think. *Then they're going to warn me that if I don't surrender to my addiction and give it up right now, all at once, I'm sunk.* As for the suggestions you may expect to find in these pages, you may be thinking, *Sure, they'll call them "suggestions," but what they really mean is that my only hope is to follow them to the letter, do exactly what I'm told, and do it their way.*

Here's our first suggestion: Relax.

No one in this book is going to tell you you're an addict. We do not hold as a condition for success that you label yourself anything at all. Our job is not to warn you of the dire consequences of this or that addictive behavior. Neither is it to blast through what others in your life may be calling your denial of behaving in certain destructive ways. We also have no intention of laying out an ironclad plan that you must follow if you want to recover.

Our premise is quite different.

We respect the fact that you're a unique individual. We assume from your having picked up this book that you have some questions about your own behavior—that you're at least considering the possibility that you might have one or another unhealthy dependency. We also know that you may have gotten the impression from friends, family, co-workers, or perhaps even other treatment professionals that you need help, but that the only way you can begin to get help is to get tough on yourself. Or at least find a treatment professional who will be tough on you.

We think you'll see that we offer no such singular, sweeping, cookbook approach. We know that any change is a process—one that must be adapted to the individual who goes through it. We offer some illuminating and helpful principles about this change, distilled from the experience of thousands of other individuals, and our own experience in working with these men and women. We celebrate the fact that you're reaching out at all—if not yet for help, then at least for some answers to questions about yourself that perplex you.

But first, who are we?

We're Dr. Arnold Washton and Nannette Stone-Washton. Between us we've had over thirty years of experience working with people who've struggled with alcohol or other drug abuse and compulsive behaviors. For a number of years we worked at an outpatient clinic in Harlem, dealing with what society labeled hard-core heroin addicts. More recently we founded and are codirectors of an outpatient clinic called The Washton Institute. Our goal today is exactly what it was in our work with the people who came to us for help in Harlem: the recovery and return to a full, productive life of every person who enters treatment.

In our treatment program, we do ask patients, from the very beginning, to completely abstain from all mood-altering chemicals and compulsive behaviors. We do this because it is only during abstinence that it is possible to learn what drives the behavior and discover what each person will need to do to recover. As treatment professionals, we believe it is important to help each individual locate his or her own motivation to quit and stay quit. If emphasizing the pain, guilt, and other consequences of addictive behaviors were a cure for addiction, treatment would be easy. But it's not. To even think about wanting a life in recovery, people have to be helped to find ways to believe it is going to be worth the effort and that the rewards are within their reach.

Yes, we believe in total abstinence. Yes, we believe that it is only a sad illusion that occasional alcohol or other drug use is okay for those who have run into trouble because of their drug use. But we don't believe that every person with a problem must call him- or herself an addict to recover, or that there is only one way for people to recover.

Many of the people we work with have come to us because they want help for an alcohol or other drug problem without going into a hospital or rehab center. Or because they have relapsed, either after completing a treatment program or after trying to give it up on their own. While we offer a highly structured program to help them battle any number of addictions—from crack to alcohol to compulsive sex—it is adaptable to every person's individual needs and provided in a nonjudgmental context. We don't play cop. We don't attack our clients. We attempt to join their resistance rather than seek by force to break it down. We've developed this approach for a simple reason: it's the only one we've found that works.

Our experience in outpatient clinics (instead of inpatient rehabilitation centers or hospitals that house patients for extended periods of time) has taught us some valuable answers to difficult questions. For instance, how do you get a patient to keep coming back for treatment?

In Harlem, many of the people who came to us did so initially because they were forced to, either for legal reasons or simply to get methadone after getting off heroin. Our job was to find a way to engage these people in a process of change—to help them want to see their behavior and lives differently than they had ever seen them before. Coercion is not the answer. It always backfires. Threatening any of our patients with dire consequences wasn't helpful; they already knew more about those consequences than we did. Threatening to kick them out of the program if they didn't shape up would have been just as unproductive. They would have been out the door in a minute, and would stay out until they got into enough trouble to have to come back.

There had to be another way. And there is. It comes through understanding and gentle persuasion. We've found certain things to be true about any person troubled by addictive behavior, whether woman or man, old or young, from Harlem or Park Avenue. If you've picked up this book, you may discover that what we've found is true about you too. Whether your spouse, boss, or best friend is on your back about your drugging, drinking, or other addictions—or whether you know somewhere deep in yourself that you're out of control when you indulge in these behaviors—you're experiencing a nagging uneasiness. It's an uneasiness you're probably convinced no one else has felt in quite the same way. No one has suffered, felt, or experienced what you have. No one quite knows how desperately and completely you depend on alcohol, other drugs, or certain behaviors to take away your anxiety, fear, and loneliness. It's inconceivable to think of relaxing or getting to sleep without a drink, of meeting new people without a pill or a snort of cocaine, of fulfilling your need for intimacy without nightly sexual escapades. What would life be like without all this? Empty? Unbearable? Or maybe simply too boring to contemplate. These substances and behaviors may be your most dependable sources of fun, relief, release. How could you give them up?

There is a common feeling we've found in people troubled by behaviors they can't seem to stop: "This is just the way I am. I need these things in a way nobody else does. I could no more give them up than give up breathing." They feel deeply alone, like there isn't anyone else on the planet quite like them.

As we've said, you are unique. But what we hope to help you see in this book is that you're not alone. The feelings that plague you, the dependency you can't imagine giving up—many, many people have felt exactly as you do. Acknowledging these feelings can lead you to some wonderful discoveries about your potential for change. And this isn't simply about changing your addictive behavior, but changing some of your most basic assumptions about who you are, what you feel inside, and what you can achieve in your life.

WHAT STEP ZERO MEANS

Achieving this new perspective isn't something that requires utter submission. We've already said that our premise doesn't include labeling yourself anything, doesn't require you, right away, to make any lifelong commitment to a completely different way of life. As heartily as we endorse Twelve Step programs to anyone who seeks support in his or her decision to achieve sobriety, we also acknowledge that accepting even the First Step, which requires that you admit you are powerless over a certain substance or behavior and that your life has become unmanageable, is too huge a leap for many people to make.

There's a lot of territory to cover before you get to the First Step of a Twelve Step program. That's the territory we hope to help you travel in this book. Recovery can't begin unless you start where you are right now. We're not saying that there aren't tough decisions to be made. We're certainly not in the business of holding out false hope that you can learn how to moderate or control that behavior rather than give it up. All we want to do is start at the beginning. And for many people who are troubled by addictive or compulsive behaviors, that means starting at what we call Step Zero.

Here's how many of our clients have characterized it:

> I am not convinced that I am an alcoholic or an addict, or even that I behave in compulsive ways. Though these substances and behaviors cause me trouble and inconvenience from time to time, I'm not sure I want to stop using any of them. Still, it might be a good idea to see if they're holding me back in any way.

This is the starting point, the first stirrings of the desire to take a closer look at your relationship with whatever mood-altering substances or behaviors are causing you trouble or inconvenience.

The good news is that you've already demonstrated this willingness simply by opening this book and reading as far as you have. You're exactly where you need to be to explore further. And the territory you are on the verge of traveling isn't only large, it's immensely fascinating. You'll learn some valuable things about yourself, about what your behavior means in your life, and about what may be blocking you from achieving your dreams and goals.

We can help you in this journey not by making it for you, but by acting as guides. A helpful analogy is to think of yourself as the hiker and of us as the guides you've taken with you to lead the way. We can't carry you up the mountain; we can merely point out some of the pitfalls and some of the wonderful views. While you've got to take each step yourself, you don't have to take them alone.

Join us as we face the mountain. Don't worry about how large it may appear. We'll conquer it one step at a time. All we ask you to expect right now is an extraordinary journey.

CHAPTER TWO

The Fragile Moment

Many books about addiction are addressed to people who have already made certain assumptions or decisions about their behavior, decisions you may not quite be able to make or want to make about yourself. You've heard about all the movie star addicts and alcoholics scrubbing floors on their hands and knees at this or that expensive rehab center. Stories of dramatic turn-arounds fill the talk shows, magazines, and celebrity tell-all books. Twelve Step programs are suddenly in vogue. You may even have investigated a Twelve Step meeting or two. Maybe you were put off by some intimidating language, such as admitting that your life is unmanageable, or that your only hope is to surrender to some kind of higher power.

The First Step of the Twelve Steps, "We admitted we were powerless over alcohol [drugs, food, sex, etc.] —that our lives had become unmanageable," may seem beyond your comprehension. It's one whale of an admission, isn't it? And it's supposed to be the *first* one you make! Powerless? Unmanageable? You're not *that* out of control, are you? In fact, the effect of all this extreme language may convince you that you're not so bad off after all. Your drinking, drugging, or other compulsive behavior hasn't destroyed you. Sure, you have problems. Who doesn't? But unmanageable? You're employed, you still have friends, maybe you're married. You're keeping yourself pretty much together.

And yet you still find yourself looking in the self-help book stacks. You may have dropped in on a Twelve Step meeting or two. You're looking for the "right" therapy. You're still casting about for something or anything that might work. Even if you aren't sure yet that the help you've bumped into applies to you, something in your life has made it clear that help is what you need.

Maybe someone in your life told you that you might have a drinking or drug problem. Maybe you're aware your life isn't what you want it to be, and you've begun losing yourself an awful lot lately in drugs, alcohol, sex, food, or your work. The word "compulsive" rings a bell for you like it never did before.

Or maybe you flat-out know you're overindulging in one or another behavior. You can't seem to get home after work without spending four hours at the bar; the cocaine that once made you feel superconfident is starting to make you feel paranoid, but you can't seem to stop doing it; the call girl expenses make your credit card bill something you have to hide from your wife, but repeated vows to yourself to cool it haven't kept the bills from mounting up.

Maybe it's even more out in the open. You think you're pretty much under control, but your boss or your spouse or your kids don't. For some reason you've been getting a lot of ultimatums lately: "If you don't stop, you're fired." ... "If you don't stop, I'll leave you." ... "If you don't stop, I'll never speak to you again."

However willing or unwilling you are to admit it, you're inching closer to some kind of recognition. Somehow you're no longer able to deny that something inside you is *wrong*. Something hurts, something needs attention. You've done all you know how to do and you're still not where, who, or what you want to be. Something keeps mucking up the works.

You're in pain, and—okay, you'll admit it—maybe you do need help.

You've reached an important moment, and it's a fragile one. At the first suggestion of coercion, of somebody lecturing you that if you don't do it the "right" way you have no hope of getting better, you'll want no more of this. At the first inkling that you've "got" to give up everything you've ever depended on for solace or strength or escape—all at once—you will probably want to bolt.

Maybe you have a history of bolting already. Perhaps you've tried to give up booze, other drugs, or other behaviors, but ultimately it was no use. You might have been able to white-knuckle it for a while. You were miserable, but you stopped. But somehow the lure was too great. You get something from drugs, alcohol, or certain other compulsive behaviors that you just can't get anywhere else—something you can't live without. How are you supposed to give it up, just like that, for the rest of your life? You're not always sure that you want to, much less that you can. And yet something is really wrong. You can't rationalize away the growing pain and despair. You *do* want to change something.

Welcome to Step Zero.

The first thing to realize about Step Zero is that it doesn't mean hitting bottom, not at least as that phrase is often defined. You don't have to be in the gutter, destitute, or homeless in order to realize you need help. In fact, some people at Step Zero make good money, hold good jobs, and sustain long-term relationships. But that fragile moment of receptivity, the first moment when you actually realize you want to change something about yourself, you want to awaken to whatever it is in your behavior that's blocking you in your life. That experience of Step Zero can be had without descending into abject poverty or misery or coming near death.

Reaching Step Zero means reaching a new kind of clarity of exactly how your behavior is holding you back. Sometimes you gain that clarity entirely through an inner process. You just know that you're ready for change. Often, however, you get a lot of help from the outside. Ultimatums from a spouse or a boss, for example. Snide remarks about your behavior that become so frequent that you can't shrug them off anymore.

The best way to take a look at Step Zero is through the eyes of others who've experienced their own fragile moments. Their stories should reassure you, first, that you don't have to lose everything before you can be helped; and, second, that you don't have to undergo any kind of brainwashing or religious conversion to get the help you need. The following stories show how family or work ultimatums, or simply an inner dissatisfaction with yourself, can prod you into Step Zero territory. The process of awakening you'll see in these stories is a very simple one, and much closer than you may ever have allowed yourself to believe.

FAMILY PRESSURES: A SPOUSE'S ULTIMATUM

Forces for change, forces that bring you to the Step Zero moment, can build up from the outside. A husband, wife, or lover is often the source of this external pressure for an obvious reason: who else gets a closer view of you than the person you live with?

Let's take a look at Greg. He had to deal with exactly this kind of family pressure. Greg is an interesting example of this, because on the face of it he seemed the least likely to knuckle under to anyone's pressure. He did admit that his wife Carol had issued an ultimatum: "Either stop using coke or get out of my life." But he wasn't coming for help because he agreed with his wife that there was something wrong with him. "In fact," Greg said, "the worst part of it is that she thinks I have a problem at all! As if I'm not in control. It wounds my pride." And Greg had, he felt, a good deal to be proud of. At 43, he had worked himself up to an impressive position in real estate. "I made a few killings early on, right after college. While friends of mine were futzing around in assistant-type jobs at law firms or brokerages, I invested a little money in some properties that I ended up selling for quadruple what I paid, then turned that over to quadruple it again. I hit the ground running and I now run one of the most successful real estate businesses in the state. Hell, in the country." Greg was worth a good deal of money by the time he came for help, money that had obviously given him a feeling of self-worth. "I had nothing; now I've got everything. Some people were born to lead the world, others to follow. I'm very definitely in the first camp."

Why was Greg seeking help now? "Actually," he said, "I'm here to prove to my wife that I'm okay." Greg was doing this for Carol's sake, not his own—that was one thing he wanted to make clear at the outset. He quickly outlined the deal he had in mind: "I'll take whatever tests I have to take and when it's clear that I'm not some kind of drug addict, you can sign an affidavit or something to that effect. Whenever Carol gets on my back I'll show it to her and remind her that I'm not a junkie." To him it was simple. "Sure I do a little coke, but I'm in control of my life. If it takes getting some kind of proof that I'm doing just fine, I'm willing to submit. I'm a reasonable man," Greg said.

Greg's facade was certainly under control. He dressed beautifully, the evident result of regular trips to Savile Row in London. He had a take-charge attitude—that was obvious from the start. The thought of facing therapists didn't faze him. Life was deal-making to Greg, and if therapy had to be part of some temporary deal, he would make as short work of it as possible and go on to his next conquest. Few people appeared as impenetrable as Greg. If ever a man was more determined not to admit fear, need, pain, or weakness, we had yet to meet him.

And yet he had asked for help. He had walked through the door. This simple fact led us to one sure conclusion: he was worried about losing something or someone. And another likely one: he felt a good deal less omnipotent than he wanted people to believe. Otherwise, why not deal with his wife on his own? Why submit to something as potentially humbling as therapy? Wasn't simply walking into a therapist's office an implicit request for help, a tacit admission that you needed it, wanted it? While his words said he needed no help, his action of walking into our office told us something different.

Greg was still a long way from admitting the need or desire for help, however. Officiously, he gave a "background rundown" in his first session. He said, "I know you guys probably want to know about family stuff, where I came from and all that, so here goes. . . ."

His rundown sounded like a business report until he mentioned his teenaged daughter, Margaret. A light dawned in his eyes as he said her name, a light and a softening. For an instant, his posture of omnipotence became transparent, and something of the living, breathing, feeling man within him shone through. "I'd do anything for her," he said. And then the moment was gone. Greg continued stampeding through his past, summing it up with the same purpose and precision he obviously brought to his business deals. Brought out into view for a moment, the man Greg became when he mentioned Margaret quickly disappeared.

Greg's father was a successful businessman. Greg's first five years were, as much as he could remember, "happy and normal." Then his father died in a car crash, and it turned out he hadn't been as successful as he had led everyone to think. He died leaving a lot of unpaid bills, and Greg's mother, doubly devastated by the loss of her husband and the collapse of her financial support, remarried as quickly as she could. "That's what she was brought up to believe you had to do if you were a woman—find a man to take care of you," Greg said. Greg's stepfather was a cold, distant man who nonetheless made a reasonably good living as an accountant and brought the family slowly out of debt into some kind of middle-class prosperity. It wasn't the flashy kind of life Greg's real father had given them, but it was something respectable. Greg had no brothers or sisters and said he often got the message from his stepfather, and even his mother, that life would have been a lot easier if he hadn't been around. "I wasn't one of those only children you hear about who gets everything he wants. Not after my own father died, anyway. My mother was too wrapped up in her new husband and my stepfather didn't have any interest in kids. So I was pretty much left to fend for myself." Which, he quickly added, was fine with him. "Taught me to look out for myself, to get ahead of the pack."

Greg refused to admit he felt lonely or abandoned. There was no room in him for sentiment. Everything in his life, he felt, "was there to teach me a lesson." And what was that lesson? "Go for the jugular. Get there before anyone else does. Win at all costs. And enjoy the hell out of the proceeds." Greg was someone for whom more was always better. He had met Carol at one of the fancy charity dinners he found himself attending more and more for political reasons. Carol was gorgeous, a svelte, athletic blonde from an old, wealthy Eastern family. She represented everything Greg felt a wife should represent, especially status.

But what about drugs? Greg hadn't so far mentioned cocaine at all, yet it was cocaine that supposedly brought him for help. When asked about it, he dismissed it with a sneer. "Cocaine? Of course I did cocaine. Everybody did." Greg had no patience for the "sanctimonious bullshit" he was suddenly hearing from the Just Say No brigade. "The same guys I knew who kept cocaine out at parties in an eighteenth-century sterling silver bowl and spoon service—next to the beluga and Dom Perignon—are now talking like they're all born again. Suddenly coke means death or something. The hell it does. It makes you feel terrific. And it hasn't exactly led to my downfall," he said, glancing meaningfully at his Rolex mainly to make his point.

So why had Carol given him an ultimatum? For the first time, a tiny tremor of anxiety flashed across his face. "Well, it's not just the cocaine. It's . . ." He paused as if to regroup his defenses. "Look, I'm a very successful man. I did not get where I am today by being indecisive. Or by not taking exactly what I wanted when I wanted it. And, damn, I don't believe a man can limit himself to one woman. It's not natural—for me, anyway. And, somehow—maybe it is the cocaine—whenever I do the stuff, I gotta go out and . . ." Greg paused again and summed it up. "Cocaine equals sex. When I get high I want a woman. That's just the way I am. And Carol's getting pissed because I'm staying out more than I used to." Greg seemed to gather himself, as if this admission was more than he meant to do and indicated some kind of weakness. "Look," he said again, "I can do whatever I damned well please. If you don't take what you want, you won't get it." Greg's words had a hollow, slightly desperate ring, evident even to himself. His eyes softened a little. "It's not only Carol," he said quietly. "I did something I'd never done before. I let my daughter down."

Margaret, at 14, had just gotten the lead in a play in her prep school and she wanted her father to be there more than anything.

"I sort of forgot," Greg said. "Okay, maybe not 'forgot.' I mean, I was going to go. But my coke contact said he had gotten some very good stuff in, and I planned to pick it up on the way to the school play. I did, too, but I couldn't resist trying some in the car, the guy had said it was so good and, well, one thing led to the next." Greg sped off to see one of the women with whom he had an "arrangement," and the night was passed in the usual way.

"I couldn't take the look on Margaret's face when I saw her the next day," Greg said. That look, it turned out, had fueled the secret reason Greg had come for help. He was afraid. He had never allowed himself to get this much out of control before. He didn't want to destroy his marriage or his family. It wasn't in the script he had crafted for himself. But he especially didn't want to lose the love of his daughter. Margaret meant more to him than anyone, anything.

"Even cocaine?" Greg's eyes flickered in fear again. At first he said nothing. He looked like he wanted to say something, but couldn't quite form the words. Then, looking down at the floor, "You want the truth? Okay. I'm not sure about anything anymore." He paused and looked up. "And I'm scared." All he could do right now was admit, for the first time, that he was afraid. And that admission, for this one moment, was a very big triumph.

What Step Zero Is Not

Greg's story has a lot to tell us about Step Zero—first by telling us what it doesn't have to be. Greg didn't experience any blinding revelation. Step Zero doesn't have to be a life-changing moment. All Greg experienced was the beginning of willingness to *admit how he felt*. That's all. To tell someone he was afraid.

We can come up with numerous psychological reasons for Greg's need to appear omnipotent, impenetrable, and in control. His isolated, lonely childhood taught him very early that the only safety he could find was safety he constructed for himself. And it isn't hard to see how the burden of making his world safe led him, urgently, to seek escape through work, cocaine, and sex.

Greg spent his entire life fleeing his real feelings, paving them over with an invincible stance fueled by cocaine and his professional and sexual conquests. The fuel worked well for a long time until Greg's need for it became insatiable. Nothing was ever enough. Nothing ever made his uncomfortable feelings go away for good. There was always more need to escape because his feelings kept coming back. And when he realized his means of escape—work, cocaine, and sex—had become more important than anything else in life, including his deep love for his daughter, he panicked. He felt what he had spent his whole life trying desperately not to feel—out of control. For the first time in his life, fear cracked his concrete defenses, his carefully built-up invincibility. But by the simple act of saying "I'm afraid. I'm scared. I need help," Greg opened the door to his recovery. By admitting his fear, he arrived at Step Zero.

Reaching Step Zero didn't mean Greg had to leap into action. It didn't mean he had to label himself an "addict" or anything else. All it meant was that he gave himself permission to feel and to express his feelings honestly and openly to someone else. The moment you say what you feel—and begin to accept that you're feeling it—is immensely cleansing. You're on solid ground. You're dealing, for the first time, with reality.

But this is only the beginning. The route Greg has started to travel toward greater self-acceptance and clarity—and toward accepting that his dependence on cocaine, sex, and professional conquests is severing him from himself—is a long one. But Greg couldn't make it to Step Zero without telling someone else the truth about how he felt. That moment of truth was the beginning of his awakening.

This moment of awakening is so crucial that we'll benefit by looking at it a little more closely. Let's briefly consider the fragile moments of two other people.

In her early thirties, Angie is a beautiful woman with dramatic black hair, a dark complexion, brilliant black eyes, and a body kept in exquisite shape by regular visits to the gym. And yet her manner, when you first meet her, is almost painfully shy, nervous, and awkward. She displays none of the self-confidence her impressive looks might lead you to expect.

Angie's lover, Dan, had been a coke abuser and a heavy drinker. But he suddenly "saw the light," Angie said. "He jumped on the sobriety bandwagon and goes to NA and AA meetings all the time. He's got shelves full of self-help books he keeps forcing on me.

"Don't get me wrong," she added nervously, "it's not like I don't think it's terrific for Dan. But he's turned into some kind of recovery freak. And I can't seem to do what he's doing. I can't seem to give up coke and alcohol myself."

She was baffled because she never thought she had a problem with substance abuse. "When Dan was getting high all the time, I thought I was the normal one. I mean, I'd sometimes drink or do a little coke to match Dan's mood; he wanted every day to be a party. But I never drank as much as he did. And I'd only do coke to sort of psych myself for a lunch date at work, or perk myself up when I felt tired and depressed. But I didn't have it up my nose all day long the way Dan did." Now that Dan was abstinent—and on an evangelical trip about it—Angie was a little shocked at herself. "At first I welcomed it," she said. "I never thought of myself as a cokehead or an alcoholic or anything. I was sure I could give it up easily. But I can't. I sneak out to do coke sometimes so that Dan won't know. I even go out alone to bars to drink—I never did that before. I don't understand it. Why can't I do without it?"

When Angie got to this part of her story she became quiet, depressed, almost expressionless. There were feelings in her she hadn't allowed to emerge. Slowly, however, as she talked about her life with Dan before and after, it all came out. "Dan has always been so strong emotionally. Even when he was drinking and doing drugs, I guess especially then, his moods determined my moods. However he felt determined how I felt. So when life was a party, I struggled to have the same good time he was having. And when he was depressed—and, boy, he could become almost suicidal—my world fell apart too." Angie let out a long, deep sigh. "I'm so tired of trying to adjust to his moods all the time. I just don't seem to have the will or the courage or whatever it takes to go my own way." Angie's tone had transformed. She sounded angrier, frustrated. "Damn it, if I want to do coke, I'll do it! Isn't that what Dan always said before he became a saint?"

Angie clenched her hands together in her lap and looked down at them. "But I don't want to do coke. Not really. I just can't seem to not do it. I feel so mixed up. Dan is at his meetings so often I don't have him around. And I don't know how to depend on myself."

How did this make her feel? "It makes me feel like I'm nothing. Like I'm a big fat zero. Like the only thing I can do is cling to someone else and hope I get an identity from that." Angie's beauty, her obsession with fitness, her good job as an office manager at a successful dermatology clinic, her long-term relationship with Dan—all were outward signs of a kind of success she felt she would be nothing without. It took enormous discipline to keep it all up. The truest thing she could say right now was that she was exhausted. It was also the most helpful thing.

Like Greg, Angie needed to say how she felt and not have it thrown back in her face as evidence of "weakness." She made her admission in a trusting environment where she felt free to talk about her feelings. While this was only a beginning, it was a beginning she could build on almost immediately. The immense relief of sharing how she really felt was so great it made her take a look at her friends and family members with whom she could share just as safely and openly as she did with Dan.

As with Greg, this first experience of Step Zero did not magically rid Angie of her desire to drink or do other drugs. It simply allowed Angie to begin to accept herself *as she was*. She didn't find a void, which is what she feared she would find when she looked at herself. She found the beginning of her real self. This beginning has become the foundation of all the satisfaction, self-acceptance, and freedom from compulsion she has gradually made part of her life.

We've taken a look at two sources that can trigger the motivation to change: (1) when your family or spouse delivers an ultimatum, and (2) when your own dissatisfaction with yourself makes you want to do something different. Greg's journey to Step Zero was set in motion by his wife's ultimatum, "Quit coke or leave me." Angie found her direction because of stirrings in herself. Sometimes, however, you can be forced into your fragile moment in much less intimate or subtle ways, like when a boss threatens to fire you if you don't shape up. Because work is such a source of self-esteem for most of us, feelings of shame are never greater than when work passes judgment on us as worthless. Witness the following story about Jack, and how he was drop-kicked into his own version of Step Zero.

WHY ME?
WHEN THE BOSS GETS ON YOUR CASE

Jack worked in advertising as a creative director, which basically meant he had to come up with terrific ideas at short notice for rich and fickle clients. At least that's what Jack said his job amounted to. "Stress was invented here," Jack says. "I'm amazed I haven't done an ad about it yet."

Everyone he knew in advertising, Jack said, dealt with stress the same way—they took something for it. "The guys on their way out, the ones who can't keep up with the pressure, seem to drink or take Valium or Quaaludes," Jack explained. "Not always on the job, but not always off it either. The rest of us—and yeah, that includes me—take something to help keep us on top. Cocaine, usually. And a variety of uppers to help with late nights, which is just about every night. One thing I can tell you, I'm not the only guy who relies on a little help to get me through the night or day. Although for some reason they're stringing me up right now as if I were."

Jack's firm had just been bought by a corporation that prided itself on its clean image and employees. "We heard that the guys who bought our business were pretty straight," Jack said. "We joked about them giving us milk and cookie breaks, or checking if we washed behind our ears. We half expected Lawrence Welk music to be piped into the elevators. But we never expected what we got."

What Jack and his colleagues got was an unannounced, random urine test administered shortly after the company's new management moved into its offices. Evidently Jack's company's reputation as a hotbed of substance abuse had preceded it. Corporate policy now decreed periodic random testing of employees, and Jack was one of the first tested. His test results, and the management's consequent ultimatum—"Either get help or get out of here"—resulted in his coming for help.

"Why me? I know that's the classic line, but why the hell was I singled out?" Jack couldn't understand it. None of the other guys he had talked to got tested, or the ones who did lucked out because they hadn't consumed anything for a while. Jack, however, had ample evidence of Benzedrine and cocaine running through him.

At 27, Jack was a handsome young man, slight, athletic-looking. He has a quick, quiet wit. He was clearly in the right business. His job depended on his coming up with funny captions and comebacks, and he was obviously good at it. But he didn't talk much at first. After the initial explanation, he stopped, as if to say, "Your turn." Greg, as you'll recall, started out as impenetrably aggressive; Angie was shy, withdrawn, and nervous. But Jack's brand of impenetrability was the most forbidding. It was passive. His attitude seemed to say, "Take me, I'm yours. Do whatever it is you do, and then let me go home."

Jack didn't open up appreciably when asked to talk a little about himself and his background, but at least he talked. The quiet recital he gave of his life was impressive—and a little sad. He had never graduated from high school. He said he hated his parents and the small town he grew up in. One day he simply decided to run away. He never backed down on a decision, he said—not then, not now.

Jack's impressive verbal skills were something he had developed on his own. He was a superachiever. From his first job as a delivery boy to his current position in a top ad agency's boardroom, he had done it all himself. He had a nice girlfriend, Susan. Someday he thought they would get married. He hadn't been in touch with his parents, hadn't talked to them since he left home at 16. His job was pretty much his life. As for drugs, they helped him stay up late at night when he needed to. And he supposed he enjoyed getting high.

The most striking thing about Jack was how little his expression changed as he recited the facts of his life. It was as if it were someone else's story. There was no connection between him and it—none that he felt ready to show. As time passed, nothing changed. He continued to remain detached from his own life.

Jack eventually agreed to join a group of five men and women who were working on cocaine and other drug dependencies. At first, he was just as quiet and withdrawn as he had ever been. But something happened as the group got going. A woman named Alice talked about her husband, who had AIDS, and how she was at the end of her rope because of trying to take care of him at home as well as go to work every day. She couldn't get anyone to help her. Even the plumber wouldn't go into the apartment because he was afraid of AIDS. Her friends kept canceling on her, making up excuses. She knew the reason why. How could people be so stupid, so cruel? She began to cry.

Jack came to life. He moved down the couch toward Alice and took her hand. There were tears in his eyes. He said he knew how she felt. He knew what it was like to be shunned, how terrible it was. He comforted her and told her he would help in whatever way he could.

Alice's story seemed to stir something deep within Jack. "She didn't deserve to be treated that way," Jack said. "Nobody does." He began to talk more about himself—the way he had felt abused, ignored, and neglected in his own family. He was still angry at his parents—an anger he had kept buried all these years, desperately trying to keep it hidden beneath his achievements, drugs, and a cool demeanor. Reaching out to Alice had opened up something in him. He was afraid, but he knew that whatever had happened to him was something he had to explore, something he had to act on. He was sick of the despair he felt—despair that until now, he felt he might never be able to express to anyone else.

THE FIRST STIRRINGS OF RELIEF

What have we seen in Greg, Angie, and Jack? What does each of their stories represent? A closed system opening up. Three people locked behind rigid fears have discovered they can express those fears to another human being. They've started to feel the first stirrings of relief that this expression brings.

What haven't we seen? We haven't seen anyone label him- or herself an addict. We haven't seen anyone make fervent vows never to drink or take other drugs again. We don't even have an indication yet that anyone's life got better. We don't know if Greg continued to allow himself to be vulnerable and receptive, or if he was able to patch up his marriage. We don't know if Angie was able to trust more in her own feelings, or if she began to feel better about herself. We have no idea if Jack continued to let out the pain and anger he had buried inside himself for so long. We don't have a clue from these stories whether or not these people even plan to give up the alcohol, other drugs, and other behaviors they've started to identify as barriers to their personal growth. If they do decide to try, we don't know what method they may use. The Twelve Steps? A drug treatment program? Psychotherapy? Or simply going it alone?

It's not that all of this isn't important—of course it is. But concerning ourselves with it right now is premature. All we need to know is that a door has opened. We've learned something about what it takes to pull the door open. In other words, we've had our first encounter with Step Zero—the Step before all other Steps—*the moment you begin to overcome fear and start to reach out for help.*

There's so much still ahead for Greg, Angie, and Jack, nothing less than a new reality. It's ahead for you too. But unfortunately it's not a reality you can rush in and grasp. It only reveals itself slowly. That's the real secret behind recovery—facing the prospect of discovering who you are and then envisioning who you might want to become. This takes time and clarity. You have to see your life as it is before you can begin building a vision of what you want it to be. That's the task we face now.

Now that the door is open, let's take our first steps through it.

CHAPTER THREE

Creating Clarity

It wasn't easy for Greg, Angie, and Jack to let their feelings out. It's not easy for anyone. Once you've admitted you feel something, you may feel terribly vulnerable and very frightened. You've not only revealed yourself to whomever you've opened up to, you've also revealed yourself to yourself. And when what you're revealing is something you've spent your life trying not to face—"I'm terrified!" . . . "I can't control my life!" . . . "I'm a fake!" . . . "I'm not what people think I am!"—it's no wonder if you've gone to considerable lengths to avoid it. You may have tried to hide behind the kind of invincible garb Greg wore, the helpless role Angie felt she had to play, the buried volcano Jack turned himself into.

But clinging to those defensive postures just doesn't work. Ultimately, all those buried feelings produce some terrible blocks: anxiety, depression, anger, fear. These are not only blocks to feeling good about yourself, they're blocks to clarity about yourself.

What Greg, Angie, and Jack finally did—and what you do, too, when you admit how you truly feel—is to create a new sense of clarity. On the ledger of your personality, you can now write something definite and true: "I'm not always in control." . . . "Certain things make me angry." . . . "Sometimes I'm frightened." . . . "I get carried away by certain feelings and act in ways

27

I know I shouldn't." As simple or obvious as these admissions may sound, they're the key to recovery from any destructive dependency you may feel you have.

WHAT ARE YOU TRYING TO RECOVER?

What do we mean by recovery? What, really, is anyone trying to recover?

Recovery or getting better doesn't mean achieving saint-hood. It isn't striving to become morally better than you were before, even if you sometimes describe one of the dividends of recovery as moral growth or moral conscience. Nearly all the men and women seeking recovery seem to be after a new sense of their own capacity as human beings, a new sense of their own potential. Their goal is a renewed desire to control their behavior. With this renewed desire comes a renewed hope that they can achieve their goal.

But something is blocking them. The reason they're looking for help is that they feel sabotaged, either because of obstacles out there that they can't seem to get away from (like bad jobs, relationships, parents, backgrounds, luck) or the more bewildering obstacles within themselves. They can't seem to become who they want to be—whether it's happy, fulfilled, serene, successful, loved, or solvent—and they can't figure out exactly why. People who perceive themselves to be hooked on drugs, alcohol, food, sex, money, or work are unhappy most of all because they've begun to make the connection that these behaviors—which they can't seem to stop—are getting in their way.

It's important to take the moral judgment out of recovery. Feeling that you're somehow "bad" or "immoral" or "consti-tutionally inadequate" provides the least effective motivation for changing your behavior. If you've already written yourself off, what hope do you have? Unfortunately, the best-intentioned people can sometimes reinforce this "bad" boy or "bad" girl sense. Even treatment professionals or people in Twelve Step programs can wittingly or unwittingly paint an awfully grim scenario in which it's your fault if you don't get better, surrender, or tow the line.

Recovery comes from *seeing* what you're doing so that you can begin to *choose* what you really want to do with your life. Blaming yourself, somebody, or something else is always unproductive because it drives you deeper into a corrosive sense of guilt, shame, or anger. Blaming always provides you with more reasons to feel that you're worthless or inadequate. Blaming paves the way right back to the behaviors you've depended on to ease the pain you feel as a victim. Suddenly, a drink, a line of cocaine, or an entire cheesecake appear to be the only way to escape how terrible you feel about yourself. Of course you depend on them, feeling the way you do about yourself. What other choice do you have?

The choice you have is to step outside yourself for a careful look at what you're feeling, how you're acting in response to that feeling, and what the consequences are—all without judging yourself. This may seem like a pretty large order. Accomplishing it does, in fact, require developing some new habits of mind. But before you can do that, you have to appreciate what your old habits of mind are. Let's meet three people on the verge of seeing exactly what their old habits happen to be.

BEEN DOWN SO LONG IT SEEMS LIKE UP: AWAKENING TO RUTS

Mary, a nurse at a large teaching hospital, is terrified of facing groups of people and dreads giving the presentations she frequently has to give to medical students under her supervision. Typically, the night before a presentation, she feels very needy. She demands attention from her lover, Tom. But the sex is always a disaster—either Tom withdraws from her intense demands and can't perform, or if they do manage to have sex, Mary is never satisfied. She still feels that Tom doesn't give enough. To top it off, she gets too little sleep and the next day is a gray nightmare. In fact, the only sleep she manages to get comes from pills freely prescribed to her by the doctors with whom she works. Since these doctors rely on her to tell them about the effects of medication, she never has a problem getting as much as she wants. These pills make her feel groggy and out of it the whole next day.

Mary is sure that her extreme anxiety is the problem; she's just oversensitive. And it doesn't help, she says, that Tom doesn't ever seem to be able to give her what she needs. She's been in analysis, but years on the couch haven't helped her much. Does her therapist know she's medicating herself? "No," Mary says a little irritably. "I mean, that's not the problem." She grows defensive: "I'm a nurse. Don't you think I know what's safe to prescribe? My anxiety is the problem. When that problem is resolved, the pills won't be necessary."

Mary is starting to admit, however, that her medication has now become her routine way of dealing with her anxiety, fear, and loneliness. She's given up trying to make Tom pay sexual attention to her, even if she hasn't given up resenting him for being inadequate. The pills take care of her more quickly and more completely. But now that she's resorting to medication even when she doesn't have a presentation coming up, the dreadful "morning after" comes a lot more frequently.

Rebecca is a secretary in a large company, but she's not the kind who wears tailored suits. She always manages to wear something tie-dyed beneath her open jacket, or a necklace of wooden beads that still smell faintly of patchouli and sandalwood. She admits to having given up some of her ideals—the ideals she had espoused as a bra-burning, war-resisting hippie years ago. She feels nostalgic for those days, even though she completely accepts that they're over. "I guess I'm a little more realistic now," she says. "I mean, I know I'm not going to save the world single-handedly, which I let myself believe back then. But we did have a beautiful dream—to get back to the earth, to fight against war and oppression and sexism." Her eyes, which are habitually a little bloodshot, glint more assertively. "I haven't given up entirely," she announces. "I mean, there will always be the Grateful Dead, won't there? And I march against nuclear stuff, and . . ."

Rebecca leaves out the fact that one of her habits hasn't changed at all since the late sixties. In fact, it has increased. She admits she still smokes grass—enormous amounts of it. This doesn't mean that she doesn't have ambitions. "It's not like I want to go back to some commune or something. I mean, I wouldn't mind making more money. I certainly wouldn't turn down a promotion here."

But no promotions have been forthcoming, not for the nine or ten years she has been with her company. One day she overheard her boss on the phone talking to his own supervisor about a promotion she had put in for. "Rebecca's too spacey to take on that job," her boss said. "She can barely keep up with the work I give her."

This embarrassed Rebecca. She showed up every day, didn't she? So what if she went through the day stoned, smoking a joint with her morning coffee, sneaking a toke or two in the park during lunch, getting stoned at night. Her job was so boring, how was she supposed to put up with it? What a sexist pig her boss was. She would really have to start looking for another job.

Meanwhile, she got comfort in her usual way. And it wasn't like she was addicted. Grass was "natural"; it wasn't a hard drug or anything. And it made her feel like she used to feel—floating, at peace, like it was 1969 again. Of course there were those nights, which came more frequently lately, when she would wake up in a panic, still a little stoned, and suddenly realize she was alone, that she had held the same crummy job for too many years, and that the Grateful Dead weren't helping much anymore. But then she would reach for the roach in her ashtray to help her forget. She would always get back to sleep eventually.

Jonathan dreads the mail. Luckily, because he works as a free-lance copywriter and generally can arrange to be home when the mail comes, he's usually able to grab the pile before his wife sees it. It's his American Express bill, mostly, although the letters to "Jon P." are also a problem—those are the letters he gets from the sexually explicit ads he places in pornography magazines. The American Express bill lists "Amanda's Escort Service" and hundreds of dollars. He knows the expenses are getting out of hand and he lives in constant fear that his wife will discover what he's up to. That would be a disaster. But he's damned if he's going to censor his sexual fantasies; they're too important a part of him. The problem, he tells himself, is society. "Why can't we do exactly what we want to do? All this post-Victorian priggishness is boring." Jonathan frequently gets into an angry rant with himself about how unfair societal mores are—an anger he only seems able to control by calling up Amanda's Escort Service once again, credit card at the ready.

All right, you say, the problem is clear enough. Obviously Mary, Rebecca, and Jonathan aren't facing up to certain crucial aspects of their behavior. They're people who, although obviously in the grip of various compulsive behaviors, aren't yet ready to admit they're in their grip.

And yet the process of coming to this admission—as you may know from your own struggle with similar or different kinds of behaviors—isn't so obvious.

None of us is ever entirely clear about our motivations or the effects of everything we do. We can't ever completely divorce ourselves from ourselves and become 100 percent objective about what our behavior means in our life, or what the consequences of it are.

This means that as obvious as the effects of Mary's dependence on sleeping pills, Rebecca's dependence on grass, and Jonathan's dependence on extramarital sex may be to us, those effects may not be obvious to them. Why? In part because so much more is going on in their minds, emotions, and lives than whatever we may think they're addicted to. And they're right. So much more *is* going on than mere addiction. Mary, Rebecca, and Jonathan are as trapped by habits of mind as they are by habits of behavior. It's these habits of mind that are the real source of the growing despair and sense of impending disaster with which each feels his or her life is filled.

Your life can't help but feel complicated. When you bring an intricate mesh of fears, assumptions, resentments, hopes, fantasy, and memories to any consideration of "who you really are," how can you clarify any of it?

By keeping simple what you can keep simple.

How to See What You're Doing— And What It's Doing to You

You may have heard the slogan "Keep It Simple" before. You hear it repeated all the time at Twelve Step meetings, and it's found its way into day-to-day speech outside of meetings. But isn't it sort of foolish? Given what we've just admitted about how complicated people are, is it possible to keep *anything* about human behavior simple?

The knowledge that some things about your behavior are simple sometimes comes in ways you don't expect. Let's let Arthur illustrate. Arthur is in his forties, garrulous, the life of the party, quick with a joke, and generous with his money. A "good-time guy" by his own and, until recently, his friends' and family's admission. For some reason, however, he just doesn't seem to be getting the reactions from other people he used to. When he flirts with the secretaries at his office, they don't quite have the good-natured sparkle he says they used to have. They're starting to look the other way. His wife is more irritable with him; his kids have started to ignore him when he gets home from work. The accounts he's worked on as a salesman are starting to cool off. He's even lost a few. "I know it's the economy, but I don't know. It feels like suddenly I'm a jinx or something. Maybe you just get these runs of bad luck. The tides, the moon, or something."

But Arthur still finds solace in his local bar. "The guys there understand me," he says. "At least we laugh at each other's jokes." Arthur refers to the bar as his "club." "It's where I go to get away from things. Like that program 'Cheers.' Of course, nobody is quite as glamorous as that. We're not all snapping back with witty comebacks. But there's a lot of camaraderie." Arthur's usual hour and a half at this bar was turning into two to three-hour stays, especially since everyone at home seemed to get so testy all of a sudden. "Why put up with it?" Arthur said. His solution to the testiness of his co-workers was similar: his business lunches dragged on longer and involved three, four, or five drinks instead of one or two. Arthur was damned if he wasn't going to have a good time, even if everyone at home or work didn't seem to want to join him.

Then, as the Christmas holidays were coming up and somebody at the bar was offering to sell a video camera, Arthur had an idea. Wouldn't it be terrific to tape the holiday events? He bet his family would have a great time with the video camera—maybe he would even bring it into the office. He bought it right then and there.

Holiday parties were big events, both at work and at home. This season he thought he would show everyone what a great guy he was. He knew his turn of bad luck was about to end. It was all a question of good attitude, he thought. He just wasn't trying hard enough to show his best side. He was really looking forward to the tapes he would be able to get of the office party and his family's Christmas Eve celebrations. Privately, he couldn't wait to see himself on the screen. He knew how charming and funny he could be—and now he would finally get to see himself on television! This was going to be fun.

What Arthur saw on the tape after his holiday parties wasn't what he expected to see. In fact, what he saw was enough to finally get him to seek help.

There was a horrifying split between how he felt he was coming across and the brutal reality captured by the camera. He was asked to list his feelings and compare them to the reality of what he saw. He came up with the following:

Feeling	*Reality*
I thought I was being funny, adorable.	People were backing away from me, trying to get me to cool it.
I thought I looked real sharp.	I was a mess, dribbling my drink all over my shirt, interrupting everyone, stumbling around making a fool of myself.

Feeling	*Reality*
I thought I was giving a wonderful party.	I saw my daughter staring at me as if she hated me—she was so embarrassed. There was no connection between me and anyone in the room.
I felt fit, athletic, in control.	What I saw was a fat, obnoxious, middle-aged drunk.

Not all of our first tastes of reality come as brutally as Arthur's did. A video camera is a merciless recorder and doesn't miss much. And we're certainly not suggesting that you run out and get a video camera to see how you're coming across. You can reflect on this split between your feelings and reality in an easier and equally effective way. You can take an imaginary snapshot of yourself at random times of the day. A sort of reality spot-check, as in the following.

- How do I feel I'm coming across right now?
- How are others reacting to me?
- Am I surprised? Are they not reacting to me as I think they ought to be?
- If they're not, why not? Am I doing something I don't realize I'm doing?

The point isn't to punish yourself; it's simply to increase your sensitivity to reality—to begin to see how much of a disparity there may be between what you feel is going on and what is actually going on.

We need to train ourselves to see reality. But if the reality that emerges includes the discovery that you're drinking too much, or that you're more adversely affected by drugs than you thought you were, or that your credit card spending is putting you in real financial trouble, this isn't an invitation to beat yourself up. Remember, it's unproductive to get into obsessive self-blaming, and it's dangerous to allow fear, anger, resentment, and self-hate to crowd in. These feelings simply reinforce the pattern you're already in by making you want to escape in exactly the same ways that caused your despair in the first place!

Take careful and honest note of what you find when you discover a disparity between your feelings and reality. Enough of this kind of inventory-taking can bring you to the moment we've been talking about all along. Step Zero, as we've said, depends on admitting your pain, but it also depends on allowing yourself to glimpse, at least for a moment, what's really going on in your life. Since you may have spent so much time and effort trying to escape that reality, it may take some time and effort before you can train yourself to see what you've been doing.

THE INGENUITY OF DENIAL

The ways we hide reality from ourselves are truly ingenious. We can rearrange the whole universe to reflect what we would like it to reflect. Mary gave what she felt was an airtight defense about medicating herself—she was a nurse and had the right to medicate herself in any way she saw fit! Rebecca felt put upon by her "sexist pig" boss and burdened by a boring job. Was it any wonder she fled to the release of grass? And Jonathan was simply living out the best part of the Sexual Revolution—giving expression to an essential part of himself. Did anyone have the right to deny him that?

It's not that Mary doesn't have expertise as a nurse. It's not that Rebecca may not be justified in feeling she's burdened by a boring job and an unsympathetic boss. Neither is there anything wrong with Jonathan's desire to have a fulfilling sex life. The problem is that these people have thrown up a screen of "reason" to prevent them from seeing what else is going on with their feelings, behavior, and lives. They haven't done what we saw Arthur unwittingly do for himself: hold up a mirror. They see no connection between their actions and the consequences of their actions. And as long as this connection isn't clear, the problem will always seem to be "fate," "society," or "my spouse" rather than something they may be doing to themselves. Something, in other words, over which they may actually have some control.

CONNECTING ACTIONS WITH BEHAVIOR

Mark, a man in his thirties, will help illustrate this. Mark was the class clown in high school. "I always had a talent for breaking kids up and getting into trouble in class. One teacher couldn't keep from laughing, though. She said I should take my act on the road. Or at least out of her algebra class."

Mark was bored at the idea of going to college. He couldn't imagine four more years of boring schoolwork. He had some writing talent, though, and he thought he might head to the West Coast and gather material for a funny screenplay. "You know," he said, "like *Blazing Saddles*." Most of all, Mark said, "I wanted to get out in the world and live." So he drifted around the country, working in fast food places, washing dishes, painting houses—whatever temporary job he could get. He went to Seattle, down to San Francisco, across to Arizona, New Mexico, spent a couple of years near Denver, then drifted back home to New York. Along the way he got involved with several women, but nothing ever really panned out. Putting down roots was for other people. Marijuana and homemade wine became Mark's steadiest companions. As for his screenplay, well, until recently he hadn't worried about it. He figured it would come when it came. He would just keep loading up on experience.

Mark got a job as a cabdriver. He went back to New York finally to write. The only job he could imagine doing was driving a cab. But the pressures were too great. People were so nasty. Traffic was so bad. The money was lousy. He began taking a bottle of wine along for the drive, at first careful not to take a swig when there was a passenger in the car, then not so careful. A passenger threatened to turn him in to the Taxi and Limousine Commission, but didn't go through with it. Mark took it as a sign. He had had enough of driving other people around, so he quit.

Now Mark was unemployed, temporarily living with his parents, and trying to sort things out so he could sit down and write the hilarious movie he knew was in him. He hadn't written anything yet, but he would—just as soon as he got his life in a little more order. Then he began to wonder if, maybe, it was all the wine he kept drinking. He had pretty much given up grass. It was too much effort trying to smoke it without his parents finding out. Maybe that was the problem. Maybe the wine was bumming him out and what he should really do was return to smoking grass, which always just relaxed him. He could go through a little group therapy, sort things out, and then be a little more comfortable with himself.

But there was something deeper bothering Mark. He had run into two friends from high school. One guy was a topflight lawyer whose successes regularly got his name in the papers. The other guy was a successful writer with two critically acclaimed novels to his credit. Mark was depressed. He had been friends with both these guys in school and they weren't that much smarter than he was. He wasn't into competition or anything, but what had happened? Why was he on unemployment, drinking wine, smoking dope, without a word of his screenplay committed to paper yet?

"It's like some essential ingredient was left out of me," Mark said. "I look at these guys and other guys like them, all dressed up in suits and walking around with their briefcases, living in nice houses, married with kids, going to the dentist, paying life insurance bills—how did they learn to do all that? It's not that I want to do it, too, but I just don't understand why I don't know how to do it. It's like I don't have the first clue how to be 'normal.' Maybe I'm just made of different stuff. Maybe something just got left out when they put me together."

This feeling of extreme inadequacy, as if some essential part was left out, is expressed by many people who acknowledge having a problem with compulsive behavior. It's the feeling that fate somehow branded you and put you in another corral away from the "normal" people.

Everyone has to learn how to brush his or her teeth, open a bank account, stand in line in a supermarket, tie his or her shoes, and iron clothes. None of this comes naturally. And yet Mark deeply believed it did. Mark was an intelligent guy. What he learned to do early on he learned easily enough so that he forgot it took any effort. Now, years later, everything seemed a matter of fate. What he needed to realize was that the ignition key had been in his pocket the whole time. What is that key?

The key is that life doesn't happen to people, life is made. Mark's lawyer and novelist friends hadn't succeeded because someone touched them with a magic wand. They learned to do certain things that paid off in certain ways. That's what Mark needed to do too — learn ways of making things happen that will pay off.

Having this key doesn't give you utter control over your life. As we'll learn to better appreciate later on, there's a good deal over which we have no control. In fact, we've already begun to see that clarity can only come when we've "surrendered" to reality—accepted things for what they are. Otherwise, how can we know what we're dealing with? What are the variables? What do we have the power to do and what don't we?

Part of accepting things for what they are means seeing that certain actions have certain consequences. When Mark smokes a lot of dope and drinks a lot of wine, he gets "wasted." He is incapable of doing what he wants to do in his life—write his screenplay, feel good about himself, achieve some personal definition of success. Mark is discovering something that may sound inanely obvious but that is a great, even profound revelation to him—every time he drinks and smokes too much he gets wasted. It happens without fail. Not once has it turned out differently! He is teaching himself, slowly, that if you put your hand in the fire, it will burn. Slowly, this is beginning to make him want to keep his hand out of the fire.

Drinking, drugging, overeating, indulging in promiscuous sex, gambling, overspending—all of the behaviors commonly labeled "compulsive"—may have certain invariable consequences for you too. But they may not do to you what they do to the next person. We all have different levels of tolerance and different metabolisms. We have different aspirations and backgrounds too. We wrestle with different fears and anxieties. But for each of us certain actions have predictable consequences. Awakening to this simple fact—that what you do has a bearing on what happens to you—may seem like the most obvious realization we could ask you to make. In fact, it's one of the trickiest. And, like everyone you've met so far in this book, you'll sometimes go to great lengths to deny this simple reality because somewhere deep inside you're not convinced that you've got a choice. Even if the fire does burn, you have to keep testing it. It's all you know how to do!

And you desperately, blindly believe that somehow, this time, the fire won't burn. This time you'll get away unhurt. This time it will work the way you want it to work. Little of this is conscious. Attachments to repetitive behaviors are so fierce because they are so deeply a part of us. Somehow we've learned that this is the only way we can be. We have no choice.

Intelligence has absolutely nothing to do with any of this. Some of the most brilliant people in the world—people who can quote you chapter and verse about "recovery" and give psychological insights of the most astonishing nuance and sophistication—can be just as bound to repetitive, destructive behavior as anyone less gifted or educated.

HEALING THE "SPLIT"

Sarah is a stunning example of this. An investment banker on Wall Street, Sarah is something of a legend in financial circles. "She treads where no man has dared to tread, much less another woman," says one admiring rival. She's one of the most brilliant analysts on Wall Street and makes a whopping salary as a consultant. Physically, Sarah is as impressive as her professional credentials. At 38, she is a beautiful woman, hair streaked with a little gray, sharp blue eyes, slim and athletic-looking. Sarah is a model of control—or at least has been until recently. In the past year or so friends and clients have noticed an "edginess" in her. But they chalk that up to the enormous stress she has to deal with in her work. It's a wonder, they think, that she isn't a good deal more edgy given the scope of her professional and social life.

Her edginess hides a clue to something secret, however. She does—and she can't stop doing—crack.

She is as addicted to the challenge that crack gives her as she is to the thrill of the high. "Crack is supposed to be for hopeless street people, right?" she gleamed wickedly when she admitted to using it. "Something you can't control, something that turns your life to garbage. It hasn't done that to me."

Sarah goes for the shock effect when she talks about her secret life. She spends part of every weekend in a remote section of Brooklyn—as far from her upper east side Manhattan life as she can get, geographically and in every other way. She keeps a cheap rented room there and buys crack on the street. Sarah's building has been broken into a number of times. She's been beaten up more than once, bruises she has hidden with makeup when she could or explained away as the result of skiing accidents. On crack, she says, she feels "free." "Sexually free too. I've picked up men on the street down there, had a really good time."

Sarah loves the idea of being a "bad" girl. At least sometimes she does. Other times—she never knows exactly when—she'll get hit by a fear and a self-loathing so great that she's more than once thought seriously of committing suicide.

"I don't know where this comes from," she says. "I can come up with the usual psychological stuff about the battle between my harsh superego and my overwhelming id and how little real self-esteem I have, but none of that helps. It's just that sometimes I feel so depressed I could kill myself."

Sarah sought help because of her crushing depression and crippling sense of self-hate. Much as she was desperately bent on proving that she could handle anything—crack *and* Wall Street—the Jekyll and Hyde split in her was tearing her apart.

Most people who come to think of themselves as compulsive can relate to this split, even if it isn't as dramatic as Sarah's. The allure of being a "bad" girl or "bad" boy, the excitement of giving the finger to all the conventions, the exhilaration of breaking free of that can be heady indeed. And what a boost drugs, alcohol, and sex can give to that feeling! "You wanna see bad? Here's bad," Sarah says she sometimes thinks to herself. The id Sarah talks about is that craving, screaming, demanding, hungry child in the center of each of us. What a joy giving that child free rein! Take, take, take with no consequences, no sense of remorse, no sense of anything but final, all-consuming satisfaction. Like that island full of candy and cake and toys in Walt Disney's *Pinocchio*, except you don't grow donkey ears. You get it all, all the time.

Contrast this with the superorganized perfection of Sarah's public life. There are satisfactions to be had here too. "You want perfect? I'll show you perfect," Sarah says she also sometimes thinks to herself. Sarah is driven to turn her outer life into what she hopes will be an impenetrable shield, a sort of glorious badge of achievement that will keep her safe from criticism, attack, and doubt. Sure, this is exhausting. Sure, it sometimes drains every ounce of her energy. But she can always return to Brooklyn, can't she? She can always resuscitate Hyde. In fact, she needs to. She can't live without Hyde. She can't live without giving herself continual proof that she's degenerate *and* perfect. Someone you could take home to mother one night and deliver to Satan the next.

The split we're describing is particularly dramatic in Sarah. But it may feel just as dramatic in you. And if the split worked— if Sarah were actually made happy by being both Jekyll and Hyde—there would be no need to comment on it. There would be no need to present it as a problem.

But it doesn't work.

It can't work because it is based on self-hate. Sarah began to heal only when she started to see herself without judgment. This was, and continues to be, no easy task for her. But it's an essential task. Recovery can't really happen until we've drained the moral judgment from it. Here, in Sarah's case, and perhaps in your own, you can see why. As long as you're lashing yourself for not being good enough, you can't be capable of seeing clearly who you are, much less be capable of recovery. You need to take steps—probably very small steps at the start—to see things about yourself you've never seen before, allow *all* of you to begin to come out, to begin accepting all that you find, and even to love what you find.

We can't do this all at once, not by the end of this book and probably not even by the end of our life. We are fallible and yet we can love ourselves. We can recover. We can screw up royally and still be worthy of love. We can slip, make mistakes, make unbelievable asses of ourselves, but still be worthy of love.

Once this begins to sink in, you'll start to appreciate that you have the resources right now to get clearer about who you are, what you're doing, and what the effects of your behavior are in your life. You can start that process any time you want, even right now. What does it take?

You can start by turning off the "judge" inside you. Turn off the voice that compares you, to your eternal disadvantage, to everyone else. Give yourself the chance to see and listen to who's there after that voice is gone.

Where Are We?

We're still very much in Step Zero territory—gaining your first moment of clarity. What have we learned about it so far? You're taking the first steps to clarity about yourself when you start to do three simple things:

1. Admit how you feel.
2. See that your actions do, after all, have real consequences—what you do does matter.
3. Don't judge what you find.

Now the next step. You may still be trying to convince yourself that this recovery business is all very nice but still beyond anything you could do for yourself. We'll learn next how to face these negative inner voices, and see how we might quiet them down.

CHAPTER FOUR

Why You're Still Telling Yourself You Can't Change

Everyone has to accept the need to look at and change behavior from time to time. But your own need to continue certain behaviors may be so fierce that you simply aren't convinced that anyone appreciates how fierce it is. The prospect of giving up your compulsive or addictive behavior still may strike you, on some deep level, as absurd. However rationally you may be starting to see how your compulsive and addictive behavior is hurting or blocking you, it doesn't matter. On a gut level you still feel somehow that you have no choice but to continue it. Drinking, drugging, overeating, obsessive work or sex, overspending—whatever the behavior, it's part of who you are no less than your eye color or blood type.

Even if you've given up some compulsive behavior—perhaps you no longer smoke, or you've white-knuckled your way to sticking to the same diet for months or even years—you may be convinced you couldn't possibly do without at least one of your remaining escapes. You may have given up smoking, but you're damned if you'll give up Valium, promiscuous sex, or your usual number of double scotches after work. How else can you find release? You would explode without having something to turn to, something to help you cope.

The bottom line—the real secret about this, you tell yourself again and again—is simple: you're just not strong enough to give it all up. You couldn't imagine dealing with all the details of your life—facing work or your mother or the supermarket, getting through an empty evening or a weekend, talking on the telephone, or falling asleep without some relieving chemical or behavior. As much as you applaud the insight Greg, Angie, Jack, Arthur, Sarah, and others have begun to develop about themselves and their behavior, they're still not you.

You're not alone in thinking that somehow your own experience is different from everyone else's. And you're certainly not alone in subscribing (consciously or unconsciously) to certain beliefs that keep you feeling alone—beliefs about why you can't change that to you appear airtight.

Let's look at some of these beliefs to see which, if any, fit you. Let's also see how you can address the fears each of these beliefs hides. Taking a look at your reasons why you can't change can have an extraordinary result. The "fuel," which is to say the fear, usually begins to dissipate when you give yourself the chance to really look at it.

SEVEN REASONS WHY YOU'RE SURE YOU CAN'T CHANGE

We've identified seven beliefs that most people use to explain why they feel they can't change their behavior. These beliefs are rarely conscious. Your experience of them is probably something like: "That's just the way I am." The fears hidden by these beliefs are often very conscious, however, and we expect you'll find most of them very familiar.

You probably feel you can't change for one or more of the following reasons:

1. You can't stand the thought of discomfort, whether physical or psychological.

2. You're too full of self-doubt and you can't imagine living your life without doing what you always do.
3. You're afraid of the unknown, afraid of what might happen if you risked changing.
4. You've got a monster superego. Your superego, that inner conscience and taskmaster that berates you every time you are less than perfect, is just too overbearing.
5. You lack the skills to succeed. You simply don't know how to give up the behaviors you cling to; whatever it takes is far beyond you.
6. Your physical condition depends on it. How could you possibly go to sleep or deal with your headaches or anxiety without your "medication"?
7. You believe in magic. You convince yourself that the desire to change is enough, thus the desire becomes a substitute for real change.

These seven beliefs are insidious, and they require some careful examination. Let's take them on, one by one.

Belief #1 *You can't stand the thought of discomfort, whether physical or psychological.*

Your first reaction to this may be defensive. "What do you mean? I can take a little pain. I'm not a baby." But, in fact, most people avoid discomfort much more than they're aware of. In fact, most people will do whatever they can to avoid it. When you discover that a certain behavior not only protects you from pain but can also provide you with a reliable kind of pleasure—or at least a reliable way of feeling "filled" and "protected"—it's not hard to see that you'll want to repeat it.

Carol is conscious of how much food has played this protector role for her. "Food was always something I could turn to," she says. "I know all the psychological stuff about equating food with love. I know all the physiological stuff about how food stretches the stomach lining and releases endorphins—the chemicals that give you physical pleasure. I've read all the literature about it. But the bottom line for me is that food works.

"For so many years I structured my entire life around eating. I made sure that when I went on a trip I was well supplied. I never scheduled an appointment even near mealtime, because there was always the chance it would interfere with when it was time to eat again. I pored over *Gourmet* magazine and all the women's magazines with those gorgeous cakes and delicious recipes. It was like pornography. I'd be having a giant bowl of oatmeal while reading about risotto. As long as something was going into my mouth and stomach, it almost didn't matter what it was. Eating was as urgent to me as breathing is to an asthmatic. And, of course, at the first sign of feeling good, bad, resentful, happy, depressed, or angry, my first impulse was to grab for food. Food was pleasure, solace, life, my best friend, lover, and protector."

The prospect of cutting down on her eating was, for many years, horrifying to Carol. "It seemed like punishment to me," she said. "What possible reason for eating less could there be except to make me feel worse? It's not that I couldn't see that eating less would help me look better, feel better, lower my chances of getting a heart attack. I mean, I wasn't stupid. I knew, vaguely, that being so fat was bad for me. But I blocked it all out. I blocked it all out because not eating as much as I wanted was unthinkable. I was terrified at the thought of not being able to give myself all the food I felt I needed."

Carol began to realize that this fear of discomfort permeated her entire life. "I guess the way I was always trying to feel was, somehow, blotted out. I got into my own version of Zen Buddhism at one point. It seemed to promise the ultimate and perfect escape, so much bliss that nothing could touch me or hurt me ever again. But it didn't work as well as pizza and cheesecake. So I went back to eating."

What was the fear underlying the prospect of attempting to eat more moderately? "It felt like being punished," Carol said. "But, even more than that, it felt like if I couldn't keep getting the pleasure, or at least the feeling, of being filled up, all the time, every day and every moment of my life, it might go away. I think the real fear was simply that if I ever stopped, I'd never be able to get enough again. It would all go away. I'd be empty. I'd never ever have enough. If the treadmill stopped, I could never get it to start again."

This frantic need to keep shoving in more and more because you'll run out if you don't is endemic in people who feel hooked to behaviors of any kind. "Discomfort" is far too mild a word to describe what you dread you might feel if you stopped pursuing whatever it is you're convinced you can't live without. The thought that you would never be able to find anything like the fulfillment food, drugs, alcohol, or sex gives you is ludicrous. But the most important point here is to identify the fear underlying the discomforting belief: *You're convinced you couldn't bear the pain of facing life without the protection of whatever behavior or substance you've always turned to for help.*

Belief #2 *You're too full of self-doubt and you can't imagine living your life without doing what you always do.*

The self-doubt you probably feel about changing your behavior may run as deep as your fear of discomfort. Self-doubt has to do with self-definition, a rocky area for most people who cling to certain behaviors and substances for safety and satisfaction. When you're full of self-doubt about being able to do something, it's often because you're convinced you're not the kind of person who can do it. You may discover that you cling to your behavior not only because it gives you a feeling of completion, but also because it reinforces your self-definition.

Peter, for example, said he had no problem identifying himself as a heavy drinker. "If you wanted to call me alcoholic, that was okay by me too," he says. "I mean, it wasn't going to get me to stop. I loved to drink. I had fun. And didn't I have good company? I mean, how many great writers or artists weren't heavy drinkers?" But Peter's drinking began getting him into more trouble than he could rationalize away. Things began to get a little out of hand as he regularly blacked out and found himself home the next morning with no idea of how he had arrived there.

Peter started questioning just how much fun his drinking really was. This questioning unnerved him. He couldn't imagine ever being any different. "Everyone at the bar missed me on the rare days I wasn't there. They said drinking just wasn't fun without me around. Hell, I wouldn't have any friends if I didn't drink! Giving up drinking for me would be like giving up living. Who would I be without it?!"

The self-doubt Peter feels runs deep. It's fueled by the fear that he wouldn't have a self if he didn't drink. However irrational the fear may seem, on some level he's afraid he'll stop existing if he stops drinking. It's not only that Peter's drinking prevents the likelihood of "discomfort"; his drinking in some sense pushes away the fear of self-annihilation. Not drinking, for Peter, would be like killing himself.

This sense of absolute identification with a compulsive behavior is common to all people who see themselves as compulsively hooked. It's not being too philosophical to call it existential dread. It's quite probable that, on a level often beneath your awareness, you fear you wouldn't exist if you didn't continue as the drinker or druggie or overeater or lover or worker you perceive yourself to be. In fact, that's exactly the fear beneath what strikes you as simple self-doubt: *You fear that you wouldn't be who you are—you wouldn't exist—if you ever stopped acting out the way you always have.*

Belief #3 *You're afraid of the unknown, afraid of what might happen if you risked changing.*

Who would you be if you didn't drink, use other drugs, or act out in other ways? While your unconscious fear is that you would be nothing, what it really means is that you would be nothing you can now imagine. This third belief clinches the point. It helps to make conscious what's really at issue when you doubt your ability to change your addictive behavior. Rationally, you may realize that you would probably continue to exist if you ever stopped your particular behavior or substance use, but you don't have a clue about what that existence would look like.

People often stick with the known even when it means misery. But not all realize that's what they're doing. Cynthia, for example, described her life as exciting and on the edge. While her friends were settling down, getting married, having kids, she was having none of it. "I wasn't cut out for that normal stuff," she said. "My idea of a life isn't sitting home washing somebody else's socks."

Fate had decreed she remain single, she often felt. She just wasn't the marrying type. The pattern of her exciting life was, however, as rigidly set as any housewife's. She spent every weekend at the same singles bar, where with the encouragement of a carefully mixed drug cocktail (ecstasy, a little angel dust, half a Quaalude) and numerous glasses of white wine, she met a variety of men and had a lot of one-night stands.

Cynthia was beginning to run on about how bored she was of the scene, yet no one was a more permanent part of it than she. Because she lived in a major city, there was no end of new male prospects, and thus no end of bed partners. A good-looking woman in her thirties, she had few problems attracting partners, although she admitted she looked best in the half-light of a dark bar; her drug taking and late nights were, even she acknowledged, beginning to take a toll on her. She looked pretty haggard in daylight, especially in the mornings when she would wake up with Ron or Jerry or Bob or whatever-his-name-was.

Cynthia's growing boredom was the beginning of an acknowledgment that her life wasn't the spontaneous, unpredictable whirl she had once believed it was. She was near to admitting she was in a rut. But she had no idea she had the power to get out of it. Living on the edge was turning out to be living on the same old edge that Cynthia clung to as steadfastly as any stay-at-home clings to his or her favorite easy chair. Far from allowing her to be free and open, which was how she liked to think of herself, her drinking, drugging, and sexual abandon were a very careful attempt to control her life. She made sure she had the same good time over and over—a good time that felt familiar, that made her feel safe in a strange way.

This is crucial. As free as getting high or having sexual encounters with strangers may sometimes make you feel, it actually represents a kind of bondage. Far from letting loose, you're stuck trying to engineer your emotions, your life, and your circumstances so that they'll turn out the right way. You're attempting to control them so that you can predict their outcome. More deeply, you're terrified of what it might be like if you really were to let go and accept life as it came, with no help from chemicals or compulsive behaviors.

It's not that getting high through alcohol, other drugs, or sex doesn't give you a certain release. The point here is that the repetitive quest for that release—for a particular, familiar, perfect release that you're desperate to recapture again and again—can keep you in the tightest bondage.

What would happen if you let go? It feels like you would die. As with the other rationales for why you feel you can't stop, *the fear of the unknown is a fear that you would be completely lost if you didn't do exactly what you've always done.* It doesn't matter that you've gnawed all the meat off the bone you're clinging to. It's the only bone you've got, and you're sure it's the only one you'll ever get.

Belief #4 *You've got a monster superego.*

A reminder of what the superego is: it's the term Sigmund Freud used to describe the inner monitor, conscience, or voice in all of us that tells us whether something is right or wrong, good or bad.

The more of a perfectionist you feel yourself to be, the greater a role your superego plays. You're an expert at self-condemnation and exquisitely sensitive to when you haven't done something perfectly. When you're plagued by that insistent voice telling you how bad and inadequate and stupid you are, it's no wonder if you've gone to considerable lengths to block that voice out.

Compulsive behavior can very effectively silence that voice. Certainly this is what Martin discovered. A pianist who accompanies singers, plays in cocktail lounges, in various pickup bands, and teaches the instrument, Martin takes no delight in his ability to support himself as a musician. "I'm not what I could be" is his motto. He'll sometimes spend evenings listening to Horowitz or Rubinstein recordings of Chopin, Mozart, Beethoven, and Brahms—then spiral down into terrible depressions. "If I had worked hard enough, I might have been able to do something like that," he thinks to himself. And he'll sometimes put himself through furious regimens of practicing, only to give up when he doesn't feel he's moving ahead fast enough. Then he'll berate himself for being lazy as well as inadequate.

Martin's involvement in what he sneeringly refers to as popular music did have one dividend. The saxophone player in a jazz group he sometimes played with turned him on to heroin. It was when Martin was feeling particularly lazy. "I thought of myself as a no-good bum who had the audacity to think he might have been a great pianist, when all I'd ever be was a two-bit pickup musician." The saxophonist told him to go easy on himself, relax. Get high. How? Oh, he could have a couple of drinks, maybe take a few tokes of grass. But if he really wanted to relax . . .

Heroin was amazing to Martin. For the first time, the inner voice (his monster superego) that told him he was a schmuck, that pummeled him until he felt nearly suicidal, was silenced. "Doing heroin was like floating away on a great dark river," Martin said. "And it felt right, too, especially given how lousy I felt about myself. I mean, if I really was a two-bit hack pianist, why not do what other two-bit hack musicians did? Shoot up." The whole ritual of shooting up, the pleasure of inserting the needle and then floating away once again, became the solution to Martin's anxiety and self-loathing. The self-hatred that had dogged him all his life went away. He could finally let go.

The swing from perfectionist pianist to heroin user and back again recalls some of what we explored with Sarah, who swung between respectability on Wall Street and squalor in Brooklyn as a crack user. Martin says he felt some of the same thrill that we heard Sarah describe: "Heroin made it seem okay to be the 'bad' boy I was always afraid of being when I was straight. I could say 'f—you' to the world. God, that felt good to just give up like that. To let myself be what I'd spent so many unfruitful years trying to convince the world I wasn't: a loser, a failure, a schmuck."

You use your compulsive behavior to escape your monster superego because you know you can never live up to it. You run from its incessant demands and cling to this fourth belief: *You're afraid to face how much of a failure you're secretly convinced you really are.*

Belief #5 *You lack the skills to succeed.*

Feeling that you lack the skills to give up a certain behavior puts a different emphasis on the superego problem we've just explored. Now we'll take a closer look at the fear you feel when you contemplate giving it all up and going it alone, that is, without the help of whatever compulsive crutch you've been depending on.

Louise slammed into this fear one Saturday morning. Disgusted by yet another sick headache from too many drinks the night before, the stale taste of smoke in her mouth, and the jittery way she felt from her morning dose of caffeine, she decided that she would give up alcohol, coffee, and smoking all at once. "I was sick of what it was doing to my health," she said. "My blood pressure was up, I was coughing from the three packs of cigarettes I smoked each day, and the scotch I drank to calm me down from all the caffeine and nicotine was making me hung over every morning. I was mad at myself. What was wrong with me? Wasn't I in control of my own life? I mean, I was a grown woman. I was 47. Surely I had the gumption and the willpower to turn over a new leaf."

Drumming herself up to a zealous pitch, she threw away a half-carton of cigarettes and emptied out every ashtray of any remaining butts, dumped the contents of her coffee can down the garbage disposal, and poured an entire fifth of expensive scotch down the toilet. "I felt like Carrie Nation on a rampage," Louise says. "Or maybe Joan of Arc. I was really doing something wonderful—something that was going to turn my life around! Who said I couldn't stop it all at once?" Louise said she thought of her father, who had given up smoking when he was diagnosed with emphysema. "Dad never complained; he just stopped. Not a peep out of him. That was the kind of stock I came from. I was going to bulldoze my way to health if I had to. Nothing could stop me."

Louise did all this virtuous disposing as thoroughly as she could. Her zeal kept her going for a good hour or more. But after the activity of getting rid of all her vices was done with, as she sat at her kitchen table looking out the window, she began to feel uncomfortable in a way she hadn't anticipated. "It was strange," she said. "There I was sitting at my kitchen table with a cup of hot water and lemon. I hadn't thought to get anything decaffeinated to replace the coffee, so all I could think of to drink was hot water and lemon—this sort of tepid sour water. Suddenly, my hands got fidgety, almost like they had a life of their own. They played with my cup and sloshed some of the water out of it. They peeled the backing off the place mat. I suddenly felt terribly nervous. It was a funny, sinking panic—an emptiness. It was a gray November day. Out the window the trees and the ground looked so barren. I felt like someone had gutted me out, taken out all my vital organs or something. I felt so terribly empty."

Louise had no idea what to do with herself. "Suddenly I was aware of having all this time, all this blank, huge, endless time. It was still only 11:00 in the morning. What was I going to do all day? I wished somehow I could just go to sleep, but I was too anxious for that. God, what I wouldn't have done for a cigarette. Just one cigarette. Suddenly that consumed me, that desire just for a couple drags on a cigarette. Maybe I hadn't thrown them all out. Maybe I'd left an unfinished one in an ashtray somewhere." Louise searched the kitchen, the living room, the bedroom, all to no avail. She had been too complete in her virtuous zeal. She looked in places that rationally she knew she had never kept cigarettes—the refrigerator, under the bed, even in the clothes hamper in the bathroom.

"That's when something in me broke," she says. "It's like I turned into an automaton. Nothing was going to stop me from getting a cigarette. I grabbed my coat and my purse and stormed out of the house to the corner store and bought a pack. I wasn't out of the store before I had a cigarette in my mouth. It was like going overboard in a boat and grabbing for a life preserver. I felt safe. But then, the next moment, I felt terrible. I was a failure. I couldn't do what my father had done. I was weak. I simply didn't know how to quit. Damn my health anyway. What I really wanted was a drink. And now that I'd picked up a cigarette, it seemed perfectly acceptable to go down a few doors to the liquor store."

This wasn't the only time Louise attempted to go cold turkey. In fact, she was sometimes able to give it all up for a day, two days, once for an entire week. But she kept slamming into the same wall. She felt she simply didn't have whatever mysterious skills were required to stay off cigarettes, booze, and coffee. Maybe, she thought, it was just too late. She was just too hooked for too many years to give it up. Wasn't it true that you couldn't teach an old dog new tricks? Well, she had never felt older than she felt right now. She felt, in fact, like giving up for good.

The fear behind the feeling that you don't have the skills to live without resorting to your compulsive escapes dovetails with other fears we've identified. What does it boil down to? You're afraid you'll fail; you're afraid you'll prove to yourself and the world that you just don't have the strength or the know-how to make it on your own. You have no choice but to grab for whatever compulsive help you can find. Like Louise, the only thing that trying and failing to get better ever does for you is reinforce what you've secretly known all along: *You're inadequate and you always will be.*

Belief #6 *Your physical condition depends on it.*

This is a big one. Remember Mary, the nurse who felt completely justified in self-prescribing sedatives because she was a nurse and knew more about medication than anyone else and knew that her anxiety could be dealt with in no other way? Never are we more fearful or self-righteous than when we feel our physical health might be jeopardized if we gave up one or another substance or behavior. "Yes, but of course I need it to sleep . . . to deal with my back pain . . . to get rid of my headaches . . . to help my digestion. . . ."

Jean was like Mary, but by no means a hypochondriac. She really did suffer from periodic asthma, arthritis, migraines, and back pain. Whenever anyone suggested that one or more of these afflictions might be stress-related, she became instantly defensive. "You're just trying to say I bring all this on myself, aren't you?" In fact, she became defensive because deep inside she felt that maybe she was bringing a good deal of it on herself. But she was completely baffled about what she might do to stop it. Her migraines were severely debilitating, but feeling guilty about somehow causing them herself just made them worse. Ditto for the asthma, arthritic attacks (which, she had to admit, came most severely when she was going through a bad time), and back pain. The only thing she could find to help was medication.

Jean went to several doctors, none of whom knew about the others. This meant that she could get double and triple doses of painkillers; she would never have to run out. She would mix pills and achieve various effects. Sometimes she nearly passed out; other times, when she added diet pills to the mixture, she would turn into a madwoman, impulsive and hot-tempered. In business for herself—she was a free-lance editor—Jean began losing more and more jobs. People simply couldn't rely on her.

She was too explosive. They never knew if they would find her nearly comatose or bouncing off the walls.

And yet, even while Jean knew that her medication sometimes had unfavorable effects, the possibility of giving it all up was unthinkable. She needed everything she took. Wasn't everything prescribed? She had the authority of three or four doctors behind every pill she consumed. She was, in fact, hyperconcerned with her health. She wasn't some hedonistic drug addict. And friends who dared suggest that she might want to seek some kind of alternative to all her pills were in for her raging fury: "Do you have any idea what it feels like not to be able to breathe?" she said about her asthma. "Have you ever had a full-blown migraine? Or do you know what it's like when you can't get out of bed because your back is in such agony? Or what it's like when you get an arthritis attack and can't lift up a pen, which means if you're an editor that you can't work? How dare you!" Needless to say, her friends stopped bringing up the subject.

Jean's life was a wild pendulum. Secretly she felt like someone frantically trying to keep a huge boat afloat—a boat that kept springing leaks no matter how many times she patched it up. Her life required such constant, exhausting maintenance. If sometimes she did perhaps overdose a bit on her painkillers, could anyone blame her? No one knew the chaos she felt inside. No one knew how hard it was to struggle to keep up appearances, how hard it was to live and work and appear normal, as if she weren't in such constant anxiety and pain and fear.

You may depend on cocaine or wine or food in the same way. You're convinced that your body just needs this kind of help. You're only giving yourself some needed rest or encouragement or other necessary aid. It's not like you're being self-indulgent.

It's not that sometimes prescribed medication for this or that illness isn't appropriate at times. Of course it is. But the reflexive urge to rationalize all of your medication away as necessary usually hides this fear: *You wonder how you will survive if you don't do what you always do to get rid of your pain.*

Belief #7 *You believe in magic.*

It's just a matter of time. Something will happen—you're sure of it—to encourage you to stop when it's right to stop. You're just not ready yet. Don't you have the best of intentions? Isn't one of the Twelve Step axioms you've heard from friends "Easy Does It"? You're just being gentle with yourself, right? Compassionate. You're not pushing yourself to do something you just can't do yet. It takes what it takes. And whatever it takes just hasn't happened yet, that's all.

But someday you're sure it will. Someday you'll know. And then you'll take appropriate measures. You're really doing okay right now. In fact, isn't your goodwill about wanting to stop almost as good as stopping itself? It's like you're already on the road to recovery simply because you want to be.

Alas, the desire for change can't take the place of change itself. Sleeping with a copy of this book under your pillow will do nothing but make your pillow lumpy. You've got to read it to get anything out of it. The whole premise of this book is to encourage you not to despair if you don't find yourself instantly leaping into radical change. But an equal premise is that you benefit from being conscious of what you're really doing and feeling it's essential to learn about and change the ways you may be kidding yourself.

Jacob was particularly blind in this regard. Actually, it wasn't that he didn't take steps to do something about his compulsions. He was completely ready to accept that he did too much cocaine, that he often got out of control sexually, and drank too much as well. God knows he had gone to enough therapists and self-help groups to be able to write his own book about them. "I've spent thousands of dollars to lie on various people's couches, scream primal screams in padded rooms, touch strangers in the dark to learn about intimacy, 'ohm' my way into stupefaction. I even was the star of a Cocaine Anonymous meeting for a few months. I was so eloquent about the rough time I was having staying off cocaine that everyone in the room kept phoning me and taking me out for coffee. I was very popular."

All of Jacob's frantic group-joining and therapy-going wasn't helping him, however. "It became a sort of game, I guess. I mean, I felt full of goodwill. And sometimes I could convince myself—when I was holding center stage in this or that self-help group—that I really was different and really was going to change. I fed on the good vibes in the room. I spilled my guts as honestly as I knew how. I made all sorts of vows right then and there that my life would change and I'd stop doing drugs and acting out."

But once out of whatever the group was, Jacob felt like an impostor. "It was all a lot of hot air. Nothing worked like cocaine. Nothing worked like sex and alcohol. Who was I kidding?" He managed to retain some shred of self-respect, however. "At least I was putting myself into therapy all the time. I mean, at least my intentions were good. I just accepted that it would take longer for me. The problem was, it seemed to be taking my whole life."

Jacob's brand of "magic"—his belief that simply being around therapy or other sources of help would be enough to induce some kind of miraculous change in him—isn't the only brand. You may have decided that you just haven't found the right therapist or lover or friend or job or place to live yet. One day the right solutions will appear to save you, make you better, cure your ills, and make everything right. But, for the moment, the sheer fact that you want to change is enough, isn't it?

As Jacob discovered, it's not enough. And the fear covered by this belief in magic won't vanish simply by wishing it away. What is that fear? *Secretly, you don't feel you've got what it takes to change. Desperately, you're convinced that someone or something else must do it for you.*

You now see a kaleidoscope of ways in which people commonly decide that they can't change, ways that, as you may know from firsthand experience, can be awfully persuasive. How do you combat them? Through willpower? Through gumption? Do you have to plan some kind of massive inner attack on your compulsive behavior like a general facing an undefeated army?

If we've struck one chord so far, we hope it's been that *compulsive behavior rarely yields to frontal assault.* Attacking yourself for not being good enough will, as you've seen with all the people you've met in this chapter, eventually backfire. There has to be another way.

We said that you can't change your life until you begin to have a vision of what you want it to be—your own vision. The process of developing this vision is what first helps you to begin recovery from compulsive behavior of any kind. How do you tap into that? How can you learn to see who you truly want to be, and thus be able to see what's holding you back from becoming it? You may have heard in Twelve Step programs that you'll change when "you're sick and tired of being sick and tired." There's certainly a lot of truth in that. But something more is true too. You'll change when, deep inside, you realize that you want to change for yourself and that you want to become someone better, freer, more at peace. That's the motivation that works. Not doing something because your superego or your mother or your spouse or your boss tells you it's right, but because you have forged your own sense of needing and wanting to change. You need to see you're doing this for yourself—that *you're* the one who stands to benefit.

Let's see how to get a sense of what it means to seek change for your own benefit. We'll explore how to develop your own vision that can motivate you to change the behavior that's holding you back.

CHAPTER FIVE

Building a New Vision

Pain is a great motivator. If you hurt badly enough, you'll seek relief. You're no stranger to the pain that has prodded you to seek relief in alcohol, other drugs, or compulsive behavior—the pain that comes from fear of the world, from feeling isolated, and from not believing you're good enough. Not that you're always conscious of that pain; in fact, chances are that for a long time you haven't been too conscious of it because your reflex action to escape this pain has become so sharp. By repeating your escape behavior often enough, you become like Pavlov's dogs. Reaching for a drink, another drug, food, work, or sex becomes as natural as breathing. Whoosh and you're out of yourself, out of what you hope will be any possibility of physical or emotional discomfort.

But as you've probably seen in your own life, the solution you've been turning to has started to become a problem. It's causing its own pain that you don't know how to escape: the pain of realizing you're out of it, sabotaging your life through drinking, drugging, or other behavior. The pain of seeing your relationships and job deteriorate is becoming an intolerable burden.

But perhaps the worst disappointment comes from realizing you're not who you want to be. The dreams you may once have had for yourself seem to have been crushed. The dreams of doing something you wanted to do, of being with someone you love and who loves you, of having a family—a look in the mirror tells you you aren't anywhere near attaining them. Looking into the mirror stabs you with a kind of panic: *What happened to me?*

Pain isn't the only motivator. This sense of longing to be who you want to be can be just as urgent a prod. The key word here is "want." As we've said, you don't create lasting change in your life if you don't want to; it's as simple as that. Wanting to can become a rich motivation. When you begin to see that your escapist behavior isn't working very well anymore and is actually getting in the way, you've got the beginnings of a powerful motivation to change that behavior. Pain only tells you that something is wrong and needs fixing. Realizing that you want to bring to life a positive vision of yourself gives you something to work toward. It gives you a reason—a deeply felt, down-in-the-gut reason—to go on and start sorting out your life so it has the chance of being something you truly want it to be, not something just left to "fate."

Sorting out Visions from Pipe Dreams

Identifying and nurturing a vision of yourself isn't only an effective and rewarding way to motivate you to change: it also can be a lot of fun. But you probably haven't given yourself permission to give free rein to your dreams, to "let 'er rip" when you envision your future. Your ability to imagine what you could become is more than likely underused, or a censoring inner voice—*But that could never happen to me*—may often intervene and bring your dream to a dead halt.

Of course the pendulum can swing in the other direction too. It may be just as common for you to believe that success will fall out of the sky, your ship will come in, and the world will wake up to what a genius you are. "Somehow," Mark, the would-be screenwriter, said, "I was always surprised—especially when I got drunk or stoned—that I wasn't being recognized, that Hollywood producers weren't getting me on the phone. I conveniently blocked out the fact that I hadn't done anything yet. I just expected everybody to know how talented and wonderful I was. The next day when I had a hangover, I swung to the other extreme. What kind of jerk was I to think I'd ever make it as a screenwriter, or as anything else? I was a no-talent bum. I couldn't even hold down a job as a cab driver."

This swing between grandiosity and devastatingly low self-esteem may be familiar to you. Your own swings may not always feel so dramatic or extreme, but most people who cling to drinking and drugging and other escape behaviors are aware of erratic mood swings. It's the swing between a pipe dream—the wild certainty that you'll be magically appreciated without having to do anything—and self-hatred—the certainty that you'll never succeed. Identifying or creating a real vision of yourself entails a perspective in which you neither over- nor underrate yourself. This perspective is bolstered by clarity and realistic hope, not desperate wishes and nightmares.

If you've come as far as recognizing that your compulsive behavior may be more a problem than a solution, you've developed enough clarity to start creating your own vision. Don't be surprised, however, if you discover you're afraid you might actually succeed. You may have a deep belief that you don't deserve the life you would really like to have. Your visions may turn into pipe dreams so often because you've been convinced that you don't deserve success. So your dreams eventually become an excuse not to move ahead. You may keep waking up to just how outlandish and unreasonable your dreams seem, and how foolish you were to ever have thought you could achieve them.

It's also true that we're often afraid of what we value. Any time we value something, we become vulnerable to its loss. So sometimes we can keep ourselves firmly planted in the misery of "not having" because we're terrified of how it would feel to lose it.

The reasons for all this are many and subtle. They spring, in part, from your own particular psychology, but feelings of being "less than" or "undeserving" seem to be nearly universal in people who escape to the imagined safety of compulsive behaviors. Deep down, you may be afraid you're an imposter, that you're not really as good as you make yourself out to be. When anything good does come to you, it's luck, not the result of your own efforts. Success means pulling the wool over people's eyes, getting them to believe you are what you're pretending to be. But you're plagued by a debilitating fear: it's only a matter of time before they find out the truth.

Do these feelings sound familiar? Again, they may not feel as dramatic or as exaggerated as we've characterized them here. But chances are you know what we're talking about. That sneaking feeling of not being deserving, that vague feeling of guilt that comes over you whenever you receive a compliment, that burden of keeping up an acceptable front. If you do feel these things about yourself, it's no surprise if you're having a hard time envisioning a new you.

Giving Yourself Permission to Be Positive

We're going to encourage you to create this vision anyway, even if, deep down, you're not sure you can change or become who you want. We're going to ask that you go ahead anyway. Imagine, in detail, what it might be like to accomplish what you want to accomplish. Then, only after you've given yourself free rein to enjoy this vision, take a nonjudgmental look at what might be holding you back from accomplishing it.

Let's look first, however, at the visualization part of this process. We'll meet a couple of people who've let themselves imagine as fully and richly as possible who they wish they were. The amazing thing to anyone who allows him- or herself to do this is how enjoyable it can be. In fact, enjoyment is the key here.

In Search of a "Normal" Life:
Charlotte

Not all visions are ambitions. Charlotte nurtured no dreams of winning a Nobel Prize. She didn't especially want to be noticed by the world. She just wanted what she called a "normal" life. "I never had huge ambitions for myself," Charlotte says. "It always seemed like some cruel twist of fate that I've never been able to achieve even my small ambitions." Charlotte said her lifelong problem was her weight. "I was always overweight. Even as a kid I was fatter than anyone else. I've struggled with diets all my life, gone into therapy and found out that food was in my mind equal to love—all that stuff. The only way my mother seemed to be able to express love to me and my brother and sister was to feed us. So it's no secret where I learned all this. But I couldn't keep myself from eating, and I was still always fat. Sometimes I'd fantasize I was a ballerina—I'd dream about that when I was a little girl. How wonderful it must be to be that slim, that graceful, to be able to leap into the air like you didn't weigh anything!"

But Charlotte says she knew that was a foolish dream, a complete fantasy. She would have been happy just to look normal. "To be able to walk into a room and have people think I looked like a regular person, maybe even to attract a man." Charlotte dreamed, as she filled her mouth with food, of having a husband, kids, and a nice home. But her dreams, even the less ambitious ones, seemed to be only that: dreams. "I believed that some people were just marked to be outsiders. I was one of those people. There was nothing I could do to change. I was destined to be fat and miserable."

The only thing Charlotte says she hadn't tried to help control her weight was drugs. "My father died of cirrhosis of the liver from drinking too much," she said, "and I vowed to myself I'd never drink or take drugs." But when she saw an overweight cousin of hers suddenly begin to slim down, she asked how she had done it and found out about a "miracle doctor." "I mean, this doctor *prescribed* diet pills. It wasn't like getting drugs off the street like some kind of addict." Charlotte overcame her fear of taking these pills long enough to make an appointment. The doctor seemed competent and genuinely sympathetic, and Charlotte began taking diet pills.

By the time she asked for help, Charlotte had lost a huge amount of weight, but she was terribly nervous and agitated and couldn't stop taking the pills. She said, "I thought it would be heaven to be 'normal,' but I've never been more miserable. What happened? Why can't I be happy now that I'm slim?" Charlotte knew that her short temper, inability to sleep, and wild mood swings were probably connected to the pills she was taking, but she couldn't figure out how to stop. She was convinced her huge appetite would come raging back if she ever quit taking her "medication." She would be fat again. But now she was even more baffled than she had been before: "It doesn't seem to matter whether I'm fat *or* thin. I'm still as miserable as I ever was."

Charlotte's feeling of being doomed to eternal ostracism and misery strikes a chord in so many people who find themselves hooked on food, alcohol, other drugs, and other substances and behaviors. But as she began to explore her feelings about her weight and her now desperate pill taking, she started to see that she had never focused on who or what she really wanted to be besides slim. The only dream she could allow herself to have was losing weight. Beyond that, she couldn't envision who that new slim self might be.

When Charlotte was asked to make a list of how she wished she felt, she was stymied. "This is all such fantasy! I could never feel what I'd like to feel." Still, she went ahead and tried: first to make a list of how she wished she felt, then to say specifically what she wished her life could be like. Haltingly, she came up with the following:

I wish I felt . . .

- at peace with myself.
- not so short-tempered with everyone.
- I could laugh and enjoy life more.
- that it didn't matter so much how attractive I was.
- free.

Now that she had broken the ice a little about her feelings, she was pressed to go further, to let her imagination run free and tell herself what the best life she could imagine might look like, and to have fun with the vision by making it as outlandish as she wanted. She looked baffled, then smiled a little shyly before she spoke.

"I wish—I wish I could go dancing every night. I wish some wonderful man would come and take me to a glamorous night-club and everyone would ooh and aah when we got up to dance because we were so beautiful and graceful." Charlotte paused and thought a bit more. "I wish I could go home with this wonderful man and make love in a big white bed in a little house by the ocean, with white curtains fluttering in the sea breeze and the sound of the waves." She stopped and closed her eyes and continued in a softer voice. "I wish this man loved me, that I loved him. And I wish that the next morning," Charlotte re-opened her eyes and laughed, "we could eat oatmeal. Huge steaming bowls of oatmeal with raisins and cream and brown sugar. And then we'd have a normal life. We'd be married and we'd plan to have kids and we'd have a normal, happy life together. We'd go to work and come home and watch the evening news and ask how each other's day was."

Charlotte stopped. "This is stupid," she announced, her face darkening. "Kid stuff. None of this will ever happen to me. Sounds like some combination of Donna Reed and Danielle Steel." She was angry. "How is this supposed to help me? I'm just not cut out to be happy. I don't—" she paused.

"You don't what?"

"I don't deserve to be happy," she finally said.

"You've lived your whole life on that assumption, haven't you?"

Charlotte's eyes softened, grew lighter. "Yes, I guess I have."

"What would happen if you tried another assumption on for size—that you had the right to be happy?"

Charlotte gave a quick shudder. "I couldn't imagine."

"Would you like to try?"

"Well, sure. But how?"

You Have a Choice

The answer starts to come when you see what Charlotte had begun to see in her visualization. It was by unleashing her vision of what she wanted her life to be that she could see a basic assumption she had made about herself—that she didn't deserve anything positive or joyful or good in her life. She didn't deserve to be happy. Once she could see that this was an assumption, it opened up the possibility that she could make other assumptions. And that what she had believed about herself didn't have to be true. Maybe—just maybe—she could learn to see herself as deserving.

A new idea can dawn when you allow your vision to come out. It isn't so much that you learn your vision might be possible—nothing guarantees that Charlotte will find the wonderful man and have the perfect life she's imagined for herself. But you get the inkling that you have a choice about what and who you could be. You have a choice about what to assume about yourself. As new and uncomfortable an idea as this may seem to you, you might actually learn to see yourself as capable of success. You might see yourself as capable of something freer and more satisfying than you ever allowed yourself to imagine.

A DREAM OF ORANGES:
JUAN

Juan's life had always been a mess. "Nothing's ever gone right for me," he said. "My father died when I was five years old and my mother had six other kids and we had almost no money. What little we had seemed to get spent on beer. When I was a kid, I drank more beer than milk."

The only bright spot in his life he could remember was the summer he had spent between eighth and ninth grades when he got a job working for a neighborhood grocer. Juan said he didn't seek the job out himself; his mother had a long-standing bill, and the grocer said that if she could get one of her kids to work part-time for him, it would pay off the bill. Juan was the oldest, so he was pushed into the job. "I hated it at first," he said. "I just wanted to hang out with the other kids and goof off.

"But something strange happened. I started to care about the job. The old grocer just dumped his produce into bins without making it look nice. For some reason this bothered me. I started to arrange the oranges and lemons and cabbages in nice piles. Once I did that, I looked around the store and saw that the rest of his stuff looked worse than it had to. He hadn't taken any time with it, and I figured he could sell more if it looked better.

"God knows why I cared, I just did. In between sweeping up and carrying boxes of cans and stuff out from the back room, which is what he'd hired me to do, I sort of straightened things up. He didn't seem to notice at first. Then a neighborhood lady came in and said how nice the oranges looked, she thought she'd buy a dozen. And the cabbages started going. He always had a hard time with them because they kept rotting and he'd have to throw them away. But now people started buying more stuff.

"This grocer guy knew he had it good with me there. He started treating me better. He gave me a little money on top of what he took off my mother's bill. He even said to me, 'You're different from the rest of those punks out there. You'll make something of yourself.'"

Juan gave a grim laugh. "Yeah, well, that was before the rent went up and the old guy had to close down. That was the beginning and the end of my business career. By the time I was out of ninth grade, I was out of school, out of work, and out of my mind on beer and pot. I didn't give a damn about making anything of myself after that. I just wanted to have a good time and get high like my friends. But sometimes I'd see that old guy walking in the street and I'd feel bad. He'd look at me hanging out with my friends, drinking beer, and he'd shake his head. Something made me want to run up and say I was sorry. Or maybe just run away so he wouldn't see me. I felt bad. Ashamed."

Juan bounced around from lousy job to lousy job—some of them legal, some not—relying on booze and dope to obliterate how bad he was starting to feel about himself. But sometimes he would dream about putting those oranges in piles and feel like crying. "It was like I was something good then," he says. "That old guy saw something good in me. I feel like such a bum now."

Juan was asked what would have happened if the grocery store hadn't closed down. How would his life have turned out if he had been able to stick with that job and create the life the old grocer envisioned for him? If he could fantasize as freely as he desired, what did he wish his own life had really become?

Juan looked suspicious. "What do you think I want?" he said. "I want to be rich, live good. What does anybody want?"

This wasn't specific enough. He was asked to go back to that grocer's and imagine how he would manage to get rich and have the life he wanted. What, exactly, would he have done? What did he now wish had happened?

"Well, I don't know. I guess once my mother's bill was all paid off, the boss would have given me a raise. Maybe he'd trust me so that when he wanted to take some time off, I could manage the store on my own. Then, hell, I'd figure out what other stores were charging for their produce and I'd charge a few cents less, make nice signs with 'SALE' written on them. Get a little competitive. I'd repaint the outside so it would look real nice, and when the store started making more money, have some fancy chrome refrigerators put in. Maybe I'd start a nice deli like they have in those more expensive places. Stock it with nice cheeses, sausages, salads, and things. Get a better clientele in.

"And then, who knows, when the old guy retires he gives the business to me. It's the best business in the neighborhood. So successful that I hire people to help me. Maybe I'd open up another food store. Maybe start a chain. Then, you know, I start to be somebody. I get written up in the paper. 'Homeboy Makes Good.' Start delegating responsibility. Make enough money to buy my own place, get a car, maybe even get married."

Juan was really rolling now—until, like Charlotte, he brought himself short with what suddenly seemed the absurdity of this big dream. "What the hell am I talking about? I sound like a lunatic. None of this could ever happen."

"Why not?"

"Because it's too late. I'm not a kid anymore. I'm a bum. I can't start over again."

"Why?"

Juan got angry. "Because that kind of stuff happens to other people, not me. Crap happens to me. Look at my life. You see anything that looks like success?"

"So you're just not the type of guy who succeeds, is that it?"

"Yeah, that's it."

"What type of guy succeeds?"

"The type who keeps piling up oranges nice. The type who won't give up just because he loses a job. The type of guy I'm not."

Just like Charlotte, Juan was convinced he was somehow marked for failure. He had assumed he was unsuccessful, but he didn't realize that it was only an assumption. It didn't have to be the truth. And the only solution he could find was to lose himself in booze and drugs. Except now the booze and drugs weren't working so hot. He wasn't having a good time anymore; he was just getting more wasted, more depressed, in more and more trouble.

Juan seemed happy when he described his dream, his vision of himself as successful. He didn't have to drink or smoke pot to feel that happiness. He could summon it up without chemical help. He could imagine himself, at least for a moment, as someone who deserved to succeed, who had a right to happiness.

Could he imagine himself that way again? His frown was more sad than angry now. "I guess so. But what good would it do?"

The good it can do is immense. If you imagine yourself as deserving, you plant the seed of the belief that you *are* deserving.

Juan needed to plant and nurture that seed, and he could do so simply by allowing his vision to blossom as abundantly and freely as possible, without censure, without judgment. But he needed to do more. In other words, it was time to look at his drinking and drugging.

This is the scary part. Examining your own destructive behavior can seem like walking through a mine field. Why? Because it makes you feel defensive, guilty, and judgmental. Imagine someone asking you about your drinking and drugging or overindulgence in any other behavior. Or remember what it was like when somebody confronted you about it. How did you feel? Did you make excuses? Did you tell the person to mind his or her own business? Or did you feel guilty? Did you say you had screwed up and you wouldn't do it again? Or did you simply shrug and say that you couldn't do anything about it, that you just couldn't stop?

Let's take a new look at your own behavior and how it might be sabotaging you. But first, take a few minutes and do what you've seen Juan and Charlotte do: "Let the sky be the limit." Come up with a vision of who you wish you were but haven't yet become. Then we'll suggest some ways of seeing what may be holding you back from the freedom and satisfaction you have every right to pursue.

SEEING THE NEW YOU

Remember, this is the time to let go. This is where you paint exactly the picture you want to paint, see yourself as the person you would like to be.

Start by making two lists. The first will be of how you feel now. The second will be of how you wish you felt. It helps to write these feelings down so that you have a record in front of you that you may want to look at later.

Sample lists might look like these.

How I feel now:	*How I wish I felt:*
Trapped	Free
Lonely	Connected
Fearful	Fearless
Depressed	Happy
Unfulfilled	Fulfilled
Dependent	Independent
Pessimistic	Optimistic
Resentful	Accepting

Now let your mind go. Visualize who you wish you were, who you would like to be in the most perfect of worlds. Be patient with yourself. Write about the life you would like to have. Put only the barest constraints on your imagination. Let yourself go. Build your vision on the list of positive feelings you've just written down and be specific about exactly what it is that you want.

Here are some questions you might want to consider as you begin to build your vision:

- What would I like my friendships and love relationships to be like?
- How would I like to look?
- What would I like my home to be like?
- What's the most secure and comforting environment I could imagine for myself?

- What would I like other people to think of me?
- How would I like to relate to the family and friends I've got today?
- Do I want to travel? If so, where?
- What kind of work do I wish I were doing?
- What would make me feel most fulfilled?

Slowly, you'll be able to paint a picture of yourself that may surprise you, that of a glowing, radiant, happy, joyous, free self. But prepare yourself for the crash. Imagining positive things about yourself is an invitation to the old censoring voice in you to roar back, "Who are you kidding? What kind of fantasyland are you living in? You think you've got the talent, discipline, money, time, and youth to become all that? Grow up!"

You can make good use of this negative voice. Instead of trying to drown it out, listen to it. What is it telling you about yourself? What assumptions is this voice based on? Write down the negative messages it's shouting at you. They may include a number of these:

- You're lazy.
- You're undisciplined.
- You're no good.
- You're weak.
- You're a fake.
- You're a washout.
- You can't complete anything you start.
- You're second-rate and you'll always be second-rate.
- You're unattractive.
- Nobody could love you.
- It's too late to change; you'll always be exactly the way you are now.

Open your eyes to look at whatever list of negatives you've come up with to see what you've been telling yourself.

When Charlotte did this, she cried. "I guess I've been pretty horrible to myself. How could I believe all those terrible things were true?"

When Juan looked at his own list of negatives, he let out a long, low whistle. Then he laughed, quietly. "Boy," he said. "I'm not exactly crazy about myself, am I?"

Your own response might be either one of these or something else entirely. But you have in front of you something very valuable. *You've got a list of what is really holding you back.* Assumptions about yourself you've been drumming into yourself day after day, year after year, that keep fueling your escape from the pain of hating yourself. As we said at the outset, pain is a great motivator. You've now come face to face with the cause of a good deal of the pain that's sent you scurrying to the "help" of booze, other drugs, or your other escapes.

Take a moment to think about your life today. Now that you've begun to see that it's your own assumptions about yourself that have been holding you back, can you begin to see how those assumptions have affected your behavior?

Now take another look at the vision of yourself you've just written down. Look at each component of it. Health. Love. Work. Happiness. A feeling of freedom.

What in your own behavior, fueled by the assumptions you've just identified, is keeping you from attaining what you've written down in this vision?

Again, don't judge yourself. Nobody's listening to any of this but you. Give yourself permission to tell the truth. You can be as honest with yourself as you like. No one will judge you or fire you or hate you. There's no need to make excuses here. You can tell it like it is to yourself.

Health. Is the reason you've got no energy and cough all the time because you smoke and drink too much? If so, don't beat yourself up. Just take note of it.

Family. Is the real reason your kids won't talk to you or you have cut off ties with your parents, siblings, or spouse because of your drinking or drugging or sexual behavior?

Work. Is the real reason you can't seem to get ahead in your job or create the career you want to create because you keep sabotaging yourself with behaviors you can't quit?

Self-esteem. Is the real reason you find yourself hating yourself because you feel you're out of control? Is the chaos you feel in your life becoming too much? Do you feel, somehow, that your coping skills have been pushed to the limit? Has the behavior you've depended on to help you to cope become more of a burden than a source of relief?

GETTING OFF THE ROLLER COASTER

After doing all you've done in this chapter to identify your vision and the negative voices inside you, the inventory you came up with should be very revealing. It may also make you feel exhausted. You may feel as if your life—as intact as it may still seem on the surface—is so far out of your personal control that the pain of it is almost intolerable. It makes you feel as if you've spent your whole life on one hell of a roller coaster ride.

In fact, you have taken a hell of a ride. And what may be looming up ahead for you is the opportunity to get off the roller coaster.

You've got the choice. You may now be getting a glimmer of hope that the ups and downs of your life don't have to be so steep. Perhaps things would be different and better if you tried something you never tried before.

Perhaps you could survive without that next drink, or drug, or sexual encounter, or cheesecake.

❦ ❦ ❦

If you've gotten to this point, you know you got there on your own. Nobody made you feel this way but you.

But what do you do now?

We're ready with what we've found to be some good suggestions. Read on.

CHAPTER SIX

Taking Action

You've read all the personal accounts in this book. You've watched people come through the tangled mess of compulsive living to a new set of revelations about themselves. You've seen them develop a new and positive vision about where they are going and what their lives can truly become. It's possible that by now you've also developed a few new revelations about yourself. Maybe you're tired.

Of what?

You're tired of tripping over yourself. That's what it may feel like, anyway, when despite all your good intentions you keep screwing up, your behavior keeps getting out of hand, and you seem to sabotage yourself no matter what you do. You're tired of trying all the time to find something to fill you, to get you out of yourself, something that will take away the pain and boredom. You're tired of other people getting on your case—the nagging, the expectations, the cold silences, angry ultimatums, and tearful accusations. You're tired of hiding one half of your life from the other. You're tired of secrets and of trying to remember which lie you told to what person so that you can figure out what to say or do next. Most of all, maybe you're tired of the self-bashing you no longer seem to be able to block out of your head: "I'm a loser." ... "I'm weak." ... "I'll never succeed."

Now that you've had a glimpse of your vision and have allowed yourself to undergo the imaginary transformation we asked you to create in the last chapter, these negative voices may be louder than ever. It's no wonder you feel exhausted. Look at the feelings, fears, hopes, doubts, and resentments you've stirred up! In the last chapter, we left you at the brink of thinking you might want to try giving up whatever behavior seems to be tripping you up. And we're not surprised if you've tightened up. *Here it comes*, you may be telling yourself. *Now we get to the lecture part. Here's where you're going to tell me that it's all up to me. If I don't do it—whatever the hell it is I'm supposed to be doing—nobody else will.*

Actually, for the moment, we aren't going to ask you to do anything at all. Nothing, that is, but give yourself a chance to change some of the messages still besieging and exhausting you. Once you start to do that, you'll have begun to change something fundamental: your assumptions about yourself. This means there's a very good chance you'll want to change your behavior to match your new assumptions.

CHANGING YOUR SELF-TALK

Take a look again at the list of negative messages we identified on page 81 in the previous chapter—messages you're probably still hearing in your head.

As a simple exercise, think of and then write down the opposite of each negative message. For "You're lazy" you might substitute "You've got all the energy you need." "You're undisciplined" can turn into "You have what it takes to do anything you want to do." "You're a fake" can become "You have a true self worth cherishing." Change "Nobody could love you" to "You deserve to be loved as much as anyone." Let "It's too late to change" become "You can always make a choice to do something different and better."

Try for the moment not to resist these new, positive messages. If a voice in you says this is a list of dim-witted affirmations you would have to be a jerk to believe, thank the voice for its opinion and release it. Turn your attention again to the list and try to take it seriously. Imagine—really imagine—what it might feel like to have all the energy you need. Imagine that you truly do have what it takes to accomplish anything you want to accomplish. Imagine you're worth loving and that you can always make a new and better choice.

We can virtually guarantee that your old negative voices won't magically go away as a result of this new self-talk. They will quiet down, however, if you gently and persistently counter them with some positive alternatives. For a few moments, they might even nod off and go to sleep, allowing your new voices more room. And when they wake up again, you'll be ready for them.

You're now in the business of planting new assumptions about yourself. As with the plants in any garden, they'll take time to grow. Sprouts need nurturing to become plants, trees, or a forest. But you can plant the seeds of this forest any time you want. You can plant them now.

Changing your self-talk isn't something you can only do in quiet times of meditation. Positive self-talk can give you on-the-spot help in a crisis. Just at the moment you want to give up, you can call on your new positive voice for needed guidance, support, and help.

The concept of all this may not be new to you. In fact, your negative inner voice may already be warning you, isn't this just a lot of recycled feel-good-about-yourself nonsense? Like all that New Age stuff now rampant in the media—visualization techniques, mantras, affirmations? Maybe you've heard all about loving-the-inner-child and following-your-bliss. You may even be able to quote chapter and verse from a number of self-help books or spiritual gurus. Perhaps, at one time, you felt seduced by all that. Or maybe it's always struck you as a lot of hogwash.

But we're asking you to do something a little different here. We want you to turn to yourself for new self-talk, not to any gurus or sources outside of you. We're confident you've got the resources to begin to change your assumptions today, right now. In time, you'll begin to get comfortable with the new, positive messages you tell yourself.

As this new self-talk begins to take root, you may realize that you would like to give life a try without resorting to your usual escapes. This realization is often surprising. *This can't be me*, you may say to yourself. *Here everybody I know has been trying to get me to stop and now, suddenly, I think I might want to stop. How did that happen?*

If that's how you're beginning to feel, don't question it. Just go with it. All it really means is that your garden is beginning to grow. The positive assumptions you've planted are starting to have their effect and you're beginning to act in ways that will nurture them.

But if you don't feel or act this way yet, don't give up. Gardens grow at different rates and require different kinds of care. Just try to keep open.

How Our Gardens Grow:
Three People, Three Kinds of Recovery

Let's take a look at a few people who've arrived at the point of taking action (not all of them willingly) to see what they were able to do next.

As different as these people and their recent experiences of recovery are, they have had to learn some similar principles to keep the good feelings about themselves growing. It's not that there's any particular right or wrong method to recover. For example, you'll see that the Twelve Step approach works wonderfully for some people, while other approaches work better for others.

When it comes to recovery, there is no such thing as perfection. Even people who have been able to maintain long-term abstinence from alcohol, other drugs, or other compulsive behaviors know that the road is sometimes rocky. This is not to say you can't achieve and maintain abstinence fairly quickly. Many people have managed to do that very well. But the shaky self-esteem, the negative attitudes, the cravings for the substance or behavior you once depended on, the lack of serenity—these don't disappear overnight. Recovery, as in learning to live life fully, openly, consciously, willingly, and without depending on outside crutches, is a slow process. Each of the people you'll meet in this chapter has had to learn that sometimes a plant or two in his or her garden dies. Sometimes you make mistakes. Sometimes you've got to go two steps back to go one step forward. Sometimes a little progress is all anyone can manage.

The good news is, any progress is cause for celebration—and can be built on. And the rewards for making any progress at all turn out to be incalculable. You'll see this as you meet the following people and begin to make connections between their experience and your own.

LEARNING TO DO IT FOR YOU:
GRANT

Grant was under siege. "My wife tells me if I don't get into a rehab, she'll divorce me. My boss tells me he'll fire me unless I put myself away." Grant rubbed his eyes, then his forehead in exasperation. "Look," he said, "I know my cocaine use has gotten out of hand. Okay, I know I need help. But I don't want to get locked up like some kind of criminal. There's got to be a better way. I don't want to drop out of life completely. I couldn't stand the humiliation of it." He had heard there was an alternative to inpatient rehabs and he wanted to give it a try. "Dammit," he said, "maybe I'm wrong like my wife, Susan, and my boss, Hank, both say I am. Maybe I'm kidding myself. But something deep in me tells me I can kick this thing without somebody locking me up and throwing away the key. I want to give it a try anyway."

It wasn't easy to convince Grant's wife and boss that there was a viable alternative to inpatient rehab. They viewed it with a good deal of suspicion. "You're going to let him wander around the city?" Susan asked. "Don't you know he'll just go to his coke dealer?" Susan had what seemed to be a perpetual frown etched into her face. She was the picture of wariness and mistrust. Not that it wasn't understandable why she felt that nothing but complete incarceration would work for Grant. She had been through it all. "I can't tell you the number of times he's told me he would quit, said he'd come home when he didn't, or that he'd pay the utility and phone and credit card bills but never did. I'm sick of it. He's turned into a monster. He needs help; he needs to be put away."

Grant's boss, Hank, had known Grant since college. He had given Grant a job and tried to remain close to him as a friend despite the obvious downhill turn Grant's life had taken. But he too was at his wit's end and felt that a rehab was the only place for Grant.

Grant was one harried-looking man. Under the siege of his wife and boss it was a wonder that he was holding out for an alternative to a rehab. Wouldn't it have been easier just to give in? But he wouldn't. He believed in his heart that he could kick cocaine on an outpatient basis, which would allow him to hold on to some kind of "normal" life.

Grant's desire to abstain from cocaine was genuine. He agreed to outpatient treatment on strict terms. The terms were that he would sign a one-week contract not to do cocaine, to engage in individual and group therapy, and to follow suggestions for activities that would give him alternatives to using cocaine. He seemed immensely relieved that someone believed that he was genuine in his desire to stop. He was obviously a man who wasn't used to being trusted.

Grant got through his first week with what he felt were flying colors. He understood right from the start that he needed to follow a specific plan to fill up his time with something other than cocaine. He also needed the support that one-on-one and group therapy provided him. He started, for the first time he could remember, to feel good about himself. At the end of the week, he said he felt immensely proud. "Susan and Hank didn't think I could do this, but look, I am doing it. This really isn't so hard after all!"

Grant deserved to feel good about himself. He had, indeed, discovered that he could make it through the day without cocaine—an amazing triumph that he had almost never been able to do before. It was obvious that he had become sick and tired of being sick and tired and that his relief was genuine. Sure, he said, sometimes he got antsy. In fact, sometimes his cravings for cocaine were horrific, but he followed the suggestion to hook up with someone from his group therapy session while he got rid of his cocaine and threw away his little black book of cocaine dealers and contacts—someone he could call whenever the urge to do cocaine hit. The point was, it was working.

What wasn't working quite so well had to do with Susan and Hank. They still hadn't quite gotten over their suspicions. Grant said he had the feeling they were scrutinizing him, just waiting for him to use cocaine again. "I always have the feeling they're waiting for the other shoe to drop. Why can't they trust me?"

Outwardly, they were encouraging, but Grant had grown so hypersensitive to picking up worried expressions on their faces that he said, "They don't fool me. I know they don't think this will last."

In fact, it didn't. Grant had an argument with his wife the weekend after his first week of abstinence. "It was over a credit card bill I hadn't paid and said I had," he said. "I mean, for God's sake, I'd only been off cocaine for a week. What did she expect, that all the shit I'd created for myself before would go away just like that?" Susan was so upset by the size of the bill and the fact that Grant had lied to her about paying it that she blew up at him. "She ended up telling me I hadn't changed at all, that I was the same lousy husband I'd always been, cocaine or not." Grant had what he called an inner explosion himself. "I may have thrown out my little black book, but I hadn't erased my memory. My main coke dealer's number flashed into my head. I thought, to hell with it. Life wasn't working any better without drugs; who was I trying to kid?"

Grant was off and running again, back to cocaine.

Susan and Hank were predictably quick with "I told you so's." "We told you he needed a rehab!" But Grant surprised both of them by returning after a three-day binge with what was for him a simple and humiliating request: "Can I come back?"

Grant said he had taught himself once again that he was miserable when he was hooked on cocaine. "It didn't get any different or better," he said. But he had an additional realization this time. Something, he said, broke in him: "I suddenly realized that up until now just about everything I've done—whether I was doing cocaine or even, in this last week, when I stayed off cocaine—wasn't really for me. It was to teach my wife and boss a lesson. I was always reacting to somebody else, not doing something for myself."

Grant felt beaten now, but freer than he had ever remembered feeling before. "What they feel about me really isn't the point, is it? It's how I feel about myself. What *I* want matters, not what they want."

The realization Grant came to is crucial. He had to see recovery as something he wanted to do for himself, not as something he had to do under pressure from anyone else in his life. And, just as important, he had to make sure his recovery wasn't contingent on anything external. "I tried to give coke up a couple times before," Grant said, "but I see now that I was bargaining with myself about it. I'd tell myself, 'Okay, if I get a raise this week I won't do coke.' Or, 'If my sex life with Susan gets better, I won't do coke.' When one of those things didn't happen—and it usually didn't—it was like I'd proven to myself that it didn't matter what I did, so I might as well do coke!"

This system of getting rewarded for being "good" doesn't work, Grant realized. "Somehow recovery has to happen for its own sake. I can't make it depend on whether my life gets obviously better all of a sudden." Once he realized this, he could begin to accept and deal with whatever life handed him. On a gut level, he realized and accepted the fact that life wasn't always going to come through with roses and a prize.

It turns out that Grant's marriage was not able to survive, even in his recovery. His problems with Susan ran too deep. Going through that divorce was very hard for Grant. But it hasn't capsized him. "I've got a chance now I didn't have before," he says, "because I realize I've got a choice—a choice to face life consciously without blotting myself out with coke. It's amazing to begin to live life for myself—to be able to consciously respond to life rather than just blindly react to it. In other areas of his life, things have gotten better, a lot better. My career has improved enormously, and for a simple reason," Grant says. "I'm actually mentally present for it! But even if I suffered a setback, hell, even if I got fired I don't think it would send me back to cocaine. Something too major has changed in me. Maybe it's just that I don't want to be dependent on stuff I know is going to hurt me. That's the closest I can come to saying what I feel like now."

There are a few dependencies Grant realizes he does want in his life—dependencies he says are not only healthy but essential. "I need two things," he says. "I need people in my life I can turn to when things get rough and I need to practice alternatives to cocaine. Maybe that sounds obvious, but it's really not. If I don't come up with something very concrete and specific to do when I feel like doing cocaine, I'm lost. I guess I'm like a little kid who has to learn what to do with his time so he won't screw up or hurt himself." Grant sums it up with this: "I need a new kind of structure in my life that I can depend on no matter what."

Grant's structure grew out of continuing group therapy and maintaining close ties with the growing group of recovering friends he's met there. Other recovering people have found different structures, but certain components seem to be identical in any structure that works. They seem to boil down to two main categories that we've briefly touched on: *getting support* and *developing a plan*.

Let's take a look at these two categories a bit more closely, starting with the support part.

GETTING SUPPORT:
BETTY

Betty lived with her husband in a middle-class suburban home in New Jersey. "Sometimes I felt like something out of *Family Circle* or *Good Housekeeping*," she says. "The typical American housewife." Like many typical American housewives, however, she realized that her husband, who had a good but not terribly well-paying job, couldn't support both of them and their three kids on his salary alone. To make ends meet, she had to work too. It was when she started a job that her drinking stepped up.

Betty always had a few drinks before dinner and several glasses of wine with dinner throughout her adult life. She didn't feel she had a drinking problem at all. "Drinking relaxed me. And it was how I was brought up. My parents always had a drink or two before dinner and wine with their meals. It was the civilized thing to do." But once she got her first job, as a receptionist, she felt besieged and turned to alcohol insistently. "I wasn't used to being bossed around," she says. "Aside from this or that part-time job I'd had in high school and college, I hadn't worked anywhere. I just wasn't used to people barking orders at me all the time. And the advertising agency I worked at had more than its share of barking egomaniacs, let me tell you. There were a lot of people getting on my back."

As Betty's anxiety increased, so did her drinking—to the point where she would have a few vodka tonics at lunch to get through the afternoon. "It helped at first. I could just sort of mentally leave when my boss started in on me. But when the drinks wore off, my resentments came raging back." One of Betty's friends suggested she go to a psychotherapist at least long enough to convince him or her to prescribe something for her nerves. Betty did so and managed to get a prescription for Valium. "Between the Valium and the drinking," Betty said, "I felt I could cope, which really means I could tune out when the going got rough—and it seemed to get rougher every day."

Betty's whole life became an attempt to escape. First, from the chaos of her job, and then from her own raging resentments when she got home from work and her medication began to wear off. "I felt like I was always pushing the 'real me' down. I was sure that if I ever let my real self out, I'd start shooting somebody." Vodka tonics increased to three and four at lunch; Valium was a constant addition. For the first time, Betty's life at home had begun to get as chaotic as her life at the office. "My kids and husband all seemed to be nagging me. Didn't they realize I was working and trying to cook and clean? What did they expect of me?" She felt more and more defensive, which just increased her desire to escape. One day at the job, after she had gotten back from a lunch of five vodka tonics and "she couldn't remember how much" Valium, she simply nodded out at her desk. Her boss came in to see her passed out over the switchboard.

"Don't let anyone tell you you can't smell vodka on somebody's breath," Betty said. "I learned later that my boss first wanted to call an ambulance because he thought I'd fainted. But when he got nearer to me he could smell the booze. Somehow he shook me awake long enough to tell me to get the hell out of there. I was fired."

Betty was devastated. She had no idea what to tell her family. It had been a long time since she had felt emotional support from them. She had one terrible memory of just prior to getting fired when her 14-year-old daughter walked into the kitchen, took one look at her mother, and burst into tears. What had Betty done to hurt her? What had she done to deserve the terrible reaction it seemed she was getting from everyone in her life? Everything seemed to be falling apart. And the family needed the money she brought in. Would she ever get another job? Could she even hold down another job? Her despair snowballed. She looked at her bottle of Valium with new purpose. It would be so easy just to swallow the whole mess of them, to just get out of this stupid life. She decided to pour herself another vodka to think it over. She poured herself another after that. Finally, at her kitchen table, she passed out again.

When Betty came to, all she could remember was that she had wanted to kill herself. She was horrified. Something in her jolted violently. Something was really, truly, terribly wrong. She had no idea where to turn. Perhaps she could schedule another meeting with that psychotherapist. Betty drummed up her courage and dialed the clinic she had gone to before for Valium. Maybe, she thought, there was something else she could take, something for depression.

"It seems like a stroke of fate now," Betty says as she recounts what happened, "but the guy who'd prescribed Valium wasn't in. If I wanted to come in that afternoon, I'd have to talk to someone else. I said sure, what did it matter? I'd see anyone I could get to prescribe something for me." The substitute therapist Betty went to turned out to be a godsend. "He knew my problem was booze and drugs. He could tell almost immediately. In fact, he seemed to know me better than I knew myself. He said, 'You're at the end of your rope, aren't you? You're tired of all that—what was it today, vodka tonic?' Since I was still under the delusion you couldn't smell vodka, I thought he was a mind reader. Something in me sort of released. I told him yes, I was tired—tired of everything. And yeah, it was vodka tonic. A lot of vodka tonic. And a lot of Valium. In fact if he wanted to know, only hours ago I was about to kill myself."

Betty's recovery began with that admission. Her new therapist hooked her up with someone who was an active member of Alcoholics Anonymous and Narcotics Anonymous—a woman with a background much like Betty's. This woman, Mary Ann, took Betty to her first AA meeting. Betty remembers how she felt at this first meeting. She was overwhelmed by the honesty in the room, but not at all sure she liked it or understood it. The list of Twelve Steps on the wall completely baffled her. They looked like some strange elementary school homework assignment. But she sat there anyway, listening, with Mary Ann sitting next to her. She wasn't sure she wanted whatever this was, but at the moment anything felt better than the despair she had felt up until then.

It's been two years since that moment. Betty stays close to her friend Mary Ann and continues to go to NA and AA meetings. While she hasn't had a drink since then, "I did fall back to Valium sometimes during my first year," she says. "It just took me a long time to believe I could make it without taking something. But eventually something in me became repulsed at the idea of cheating with Valium. I guess I knew I wasn't giving myself a chance, a real chance to see if I could handle life without chemical help. I knew deep inside that I'd find a deeper relief if I could manage to give it all up. Mary Ann had been through what I'd been through, hadn't she? She'd been hooked on alcohol and downers, too, and she'd managed to get off both. I finally was able to be honest with her about taking Valium. Her response was totally nonjudgmental. She just said, 'Where do you keep it?' She helped me get rid of all my pill bottles. She stood by me the whole way."

Betty goes to AA and NA meetings fairly regularly. She recognizes she needs continuing support. "But my main support turns out to be, amazingly, my family," she says. "Once they saw I was serious about getting better, they almost fell over each other in their desire to help me. My husband banned liquor from the house. He'd never especially liked to drink, so it wasn't a loss for him. He and my kids went to Al-Anon—the Twelve Step program for people who are involved with alcoholics. I feel a kind of love from them, from my friend Mary Ann, and from the therapist I'm still going to, love that I could never have imagined before. It's like it was waiting for me all the time but I was too frightened or full of myself or closed off to receive it. One day, one moment at a time, I'm letting down my guard, and I'm letting that love in."

The result? "Life has a kind of meaning right now I never thought it could have. Sometimes I wish I could go back in time to the woman I was, that terribly sick and despondent woman, and let her know there was another way. I wish I could have learned more quickly what I know now. But I guess I had to go through what I had to go through to get where I am today. As I keep hearing in AA, 'It takes what it takes.'"

What it especially takes is realizing you can't do all this on your own. You do need support. You do need other people to call, to stand by you, to give you the love and understanding and strength you may not always be able to give yourself. Getting that support can happen in a variety of ways. Sometimes it can come from a therapist, a friend, or a member of your family. AA, NA, and other Twelve Step programs work wonderfully for many people. Betty says she sometimes can't buy the AA line across the board. "I'm not sure I can always agree that I'm completely powerless," she says, "and sometimes I find the Higher Power talk a little hard to take." But you can find people there to connect with who know the pain you've been through and who also know firsthand the pain and difficulty, and immense joy and reward, of sticking to sobriety.

Support can come from the most surprising quarters. Some people who don't go to Twelve Step programs have managed to find needed support in friends and family, or as Grant did, through people they've met in group therapy or other self-help or therapeutic networks. The point is, some kind of reliable support seems to be crucial. People who have managed to sustain successful recovery from any kind of compulsive behavior have a strong, reliable support system they make regular use of. They've got people in their lives they can trust and depend on for understanding and help—people they can talk to when things get rough.

But once you've found that support, you need to supplement it with something equally important—a plan of action. If you've already tried to give up a compulsive behavior, you know well what a shock it is to suddenly have so much time on your hands—time you had always spent acting out that now can seem terribly unwieldy. What do you do now that you're not in a bar, gorging on food, acting out sexually, going wild with your credit cards, or hunting down your drug dealer?

Learning to fill that time satisfyingly and effectively is a crucial task. It's what the second essential component of recovery, *developing a plan*, is all about.

DEVELOPING A PLAN:
SUZANNE

Suzanne is an attractive, dark-haired, plump woman in her early thirties. Her large eyes seem to take everything in; there's a kind of childlike vulnerability that seems to broadcast to the world that she's fragile and easily hurt. "I've always been so thin-skinned," she said. "The least slight or criticism from anybody and I withdraw, like some kind of hypersensitive plant that closes up its leaves when you touch it."

Suzanne said this natural terror she had wasn't helped much by the fact that she had gone through her life overweight. She said she was a good twenty-five pounds over the weight she ought to be. But that was nothing compared to what she used to look like. She rummaged through her purse for a moment and pulled out a battered black-and-white photograph of an obese, shy-looking teenager. "That's who I was. It's who I still feel like inside." Suzanne had been on every conceivable diet; some had worked for a while, none for very long. A friend had suggested she go to Overeaters Anonymous, but that wasn't working. "All going to those meetings has done so far is make me want to eat! I don't know, all that talk about food—and food plans—it just triggers a desire to eat more, not less."

But that wasn't her only problem. Something new and frightening had begun to happen and she didn't know who to turn to.

"It's sex," she said quietly, then gave a long sigh. "Who would have thought it? I've always been the good, overweight little Catholic girl you could count on to do the right thing. But I'm sick of doing the right thing. I'm sick of dieting. I'm sick of depriving myself of food—and men. People look at me and don't think I have sexual desires. Well, they're wrong. I do have desires. Look, I don't think any man will ever want to marry me. But every man wants sex, even with someone like me." She said she had started hanging out at singles bars and answering ads, not the "nice" ads for long walks on the beach, but the ads looking for "afternoon fun."

Part of gearing up for her increasingly frequent sexual encounters meant getting high on marijuana. She wasn't sure why she had decided on pot. "I think it's because the only time I can remember being happy was back in college when everyone was smoking pot. I didn't feel so out of things when I was high. And of course it made me want to eat, which I loved because when I ate while I was high I didn't feel guilty."

Suzanne also associated pot with the only romantic encounter she ever had in her college days. "This guy thought I was something out of a Peter Paul Rubens painting, and he begged me to go to bed with him. I was so high and out of it, I said sure. He was also high and out of it, so the lovemaking didn't amount to much. But I was thrilled. Somebody wanted me!" But pot hadn't given her much joy recently.

"I'm living this incredibly double life," she said, "and I'm exhausted. I'm starting to hate myself. It's like I'm two different people and somehow both are strangers. I work as a librarian during the day and spend more and more nights, even weeknights, at bars and in strange men's apartments." She began to cry. "What's wrong with me? I can't tell you how I hate myself on all those mornings after. But I can't seem to stop. The food, the pot, the sex—sometimes it feels like there's nothing I'm not hooked on! It's all out of control. All I know right now is I can't stand whoever it is I've become. And nothing's working anymore! Nothing is getting me out of myself. These days I'm not even getting picked up very much. Maybe it's because I'm too familiar. Or maybe even those desperate guys can see how desperate I am and they're starting to stay away."

Suzanne's life seemed to have become one giant trigger. "Anything the least bit negative that happens in my working day, like whenever anyone snaps back at me, when I can't get through to someone on the phone, or when the guy at the coffee place I go in the mornings seems to be taking longer than usual—everything is like a little trigger bringing me back to the same message—'Smoke a joint!' There's a vacant lot in back of the library where I'll go to smoke during the day; it helps me blank out and make it until five o'clock when I can get the hell away, smoke some more, and see who I can end up in bed with." Sometimes when Suzanne became especially disgusted with herself, she tried to stop smoking marijuana, acting out sexually, and pigging out on food, but it didn't last. She always felt like bursting out of her skin. "It's as though I've got some inner air-raid siren going on when I feel the least bit uncomfortable, a wailing siren that keeps screaming at me, 'Escape! Escape! Get the hell out of here!'"

When it came to Twelve Step groups, Suzanne's reaction was quick and vehement. "Don't hand me any of that Higher Power, surrender to your powerlessness stuff, okay?" Suzanne said she couldn't help it, but every OA meeting she had been to and the two or three NA meetings reminded her of the "hogwash" she had to swallow growing up Catholic. "I have such raging resentments against having to be a 'good' girl. I don't know what will help me, but that's sure not going to. At least not now."

Suzanne said she needed what she called "practical" help. "I really want to quit all this," she said. "But I don't know how.

Every time I try, I go out of my mind. What am I supposed to do instead of smoking dope? What do I do with my nights? How can I learn how to eat like a normal person?"

It was suggested that she didn't have to solve it all right now. She might begin to look first at whatever behavior seemed to trigger all the others. By now, it was clear to her that pot was the main trigger. "Once I smoke, I want to eat and have sex. It makes me want to fill myself completely in the quickest ways I can find." As with Grant, Suzanne started working on finding support. This included group therapy and hooking up with someone who would help her get rid of her pot and pot paraphernalia. It also included a specific plan of alternatives she could turn to when the urge to smoke hit.

Suzanne was apprehensive about all this, especially the therapy part, which she feared was just going to be more God talk or someone berating her for her lack of willpower. But it turned out that the therapy was what she took to most easily. She enjoyed being able to spill out her pain in a supportive environment. And she did hook up with a few people she felt she could trust who did help her get rid of her considerable stash of pot and rolling papers. But the plan of action seemed a little silly to her.

"I'm really not a child," she said. "I mean, now that I know I can call a therapist and the friends I've met in group, I'll be okay." Suzanne did, in fact, feel better about herself. And she was so exhausted from her late nights out that for the first few days of abstinence from pot she was able simply to go to sleep when she got home from work. It was such a vast relief to give up her nightly excesses that, physically, her body seemed to be grateful for the letup.

But as she started to feel better physically and her energy began to return, the phone calls she was regularly making to other recovering friends weren't enough. As raw and vulnerable as she was feeling now that she wasn't blocking out her emotions with pot, she overreacted when one of her phone mates asked her to call a little less often in the afternoon because it interfered with her work.

All the feelings she had of being rejected flooded back. "It was horrible," Suzanne said. "It felt as if everything I'd tried to do for myself toppled like a house of cards." Nobody really cared about her, Suzanne decided. She was alone, and she would always be alone. That was the simple, hard truth. So why couldn't she get whatever meager pleasure out of existence she could scratch out?

Suzanne dialed her drug dealer and arranged to get more grass.

But the despair came back much more quickly now than it ever had before. Friends she had made at group therapy kept trying to call her. At first she ignored the phone. Then, after two days of nearly constant ringing, she finally relented and answered. "I don't know why I didn't take the receiver off the hook—maybe I was testing them to see if they'd keep calling. Thank God I had put some effort into the support part of all this," Suzanne says now. "At least somebody was trying to get through to me." Suzanne spilled out her pain to this friend, who then came over to help her get rid of all traces of this latest batch of marijuana. But this friend did something else. She told her about her own plan, something that went beyond picking up the phone whenever things got rough. Important as that kind of reaching out was, it wasn't enough.

Suzanne learned that the triggers she had confessed to feeling were very instructive, but they were really only the beginning of what she needed to become conscious of. She learned she had set up her return to smoking grass. To keep from setting herself up again, she needed to identify the things that triggered her desire to escape.

With her friend's help, Suzanne was able to write down a whole list of triggers. "It was almost funny," Suzanne said. "I mean, there was almost nothing in my life that wasn't a trigger! Anything that caused me anxiety—if the mail was late, a friend didn't call me back, a salesperson was inattentive—anything like that sent me in search of escape. But other things were triggers too—like walking home from work past the street where my biggest drug contact lived. I didn't realize I was putting myself in a dangerous place. I needed to come up with an alternate route home that wouldn't make me think 'pot.'"

The nights were the hardest. "I had to come up with specific options, not simply tell myself to go home and read a book. That wouldn't work. I had to create an inviting scenario: go home, take a bubble bath, make yourself some spaghetti, watch your favorite sit-com, and read three chapters of the romance novel you bought yesterday. It had to be very concrete. And it had to be something I wanted to do. I'm teaching myself that there are other real ways I can get pleasure out of life. Ways that won't sabotage me."

Suzanne laughs a little. "Okay, I know about the spaghetti part. And it's true I eat more. I'm still eating more than I probably ought to be eating. But like my friend Andrea says, 'Deal with your addictions in the order they'll kill you.' And I know pot is the real trigger. When I smoke, I go nuts. I want to act out in every way."

Suzanne has learned that she has to reprogram herself, not in some arbitrary way, not in a way imposed on her by some outside source, but in a way that can allow her to enjoy her life as much as she can without resorting to pot. This means coming up with a specific plan. "It's amazing what this has opened up for me," Suzanne said. "I think I always believed that, somehow, nobody had control of their lives. It was all fate. Some people were just born lucky, some weren't. And, up until now, I've always thought of myself as one of the unlucky ones. But now I'm not so sure. Today I've decided to do certain things in my life and I'm actually, one step at a time, doing them!"

One of the things Suzanne has done is to return to Twelve Step programs. Now that she's not so full of resentment and rage, she's able to get more out of them. "They say, 'Take what you can and leave the rest.' So what I take is the fellowship—the social opportunities, really—the people I keep meeting who understand exactly what I'm going through. It's not that I don't feel despair anymore. Believe me, I do. In some ways or at some times more than ever before. I mean, I'm *feeling* things now. But I've learned something amazing: feelings pass. New ones take their place. Slowly, the universe seems to be a lot more buoyant and a lot less threatening than it seemed before. It's getting better."

Again, not all of Suzanne's troubles have magically disappeared. She wants to deal with her eating obsessions more effectively than she's been able to so far, but the success she's had in staying off pot has increased her self-esteem so much that she's discovering she isn't acting out with food to the degree she had before. And the whole mess of sex and romance is something she's simply needed to shelve for the time being. "I have to take care of me first," she says. "I have faith that the rest will come to some kind of order eventually. Thank God I don't feel I've got to solve everything right now."

Support and a plan. Identifying triggers. Becoming conscious. We've only begun to touch on ways people have learned to accomplish these things. It isn't our goal to map out for you the kind of specific plan and support network that Grant, Betty, and Suzanne have managed to develop for themselves. Number one, we couldn't. As you can see from the stories you've read in this book, a recovery plan has to fit the person who wants to recover. What might be right for him or her may not work for you.

But there are a few good pointers we can offer about assessing what might be right for you. In fact, now's a good time to pass them on.

THE RIGHT KIND OF RECOVERY FOR YOU

The most important word here is *willingness*.

Don't cut off your options before you've really tried them. Think of your attempt to recover as an adventure—a trial-and-error process that will always be instructive, even if everything you do or hear doesn't instantly strike you as perfect, even if it doesn't especially make a lot of sense at first.

Try on a few Twelve Step meetings for size. Give them a chance. Don't run out in a huff because you've heard one or another person say something with which you disagree, or because this or that Step or slogan seems to be nonsense. Try to listen without judging. If nothing else, look at meetings as a way to meet people to talk to. Trust your own instincts about who to hook up with and who not to. Something in you will probably click when you meet the recovering man or woman who seems to have an inside track on the kind of recovery you would like for yourself.

Or, if that doesn't feel comfortable, investigate outpatient clinics. Look for therapists with experience in treating your particular brand of addiction. Again, trust your instincts. If you feel coerced into a kind of therapy that deep down you feel isn't right for you, remember you can always say no. You don't have to do anything you don't want to do. It's true that many treatment professionals can come on like gangbusters. Recovery is something many feel passionately about, and you may run into a lot of "do-it-my-way-or-die" zealots with whom you feel very uncomfortable. Whatever you do, don't stop looking. Your desire to recover will eventually hook you up with the right therapist or program.

If you start out with a therapist or program that doesn't pan out for you, you have the right to leave. But do yourself the service of terminating thoughtfully, and don't slam doors behind you. What may not work for you now may work for you in the future. Remember, Suzanne was turned off by Twelve Step programs early in her attempts to recover, but she was able to participate in them later on with great satisfaction.

Our main message is this: you have options. From Twelve Step programs, to one-on-one therapy, to the kind of outpatient care provided by clinics like our own, to the support and strength you can sometimes get from family and friends—the world is abundant with sources of help.

Is recovery easy? Rarely. Is it worth it? It seems to be. Many people who were once miserable when they felt hooked on alcohol, other drugs, or other behaviors have begun to taste what life is like when it's lived consciously.

But sometimes consciousness is frightening. When you're used to fleeing the reality of your feelings, it's not easy to change gears and be present for everything. "I've never been awake so much," says one recovering addict. "It's no wonder I go to bed at eight o'clock at night. I've never received so much stimulus, so much life before. I'm exhausted."

This sudden onslaught of life is revealing and often wonderful, but it can feel overwhelming. Like Grant, Betty, and Suzanne, there may be times when you get to a point of such resentment or despair that you're convinced you can't do without some escape, a retreat to your old ways of getting high and getting away.

What happens then? Are you lost? Have you failed utterly? Is there any point in trying to recover again?

Learning how to live life consciously means learning how to live and deal with disappointment. And sometimes that disappointment comes in the form of what is commonly referred to as a "slip." Nobody has to slip. But if it happens, it doesn't have to be the end of the world. Exploring what a slip really is, and what to do if you have one, means traveling some important and surprising territory—territory you need to travel to get the best chance of living a conscious life without capsizing.

CHAPTER SEVEN

Dealing with Disappointment

People who are overwhelmed with enthusiasm for recovery—the Gung ho! crowd—worry us sometimes. For all their zeal, these are the people whose prospects for long-term sobriety often turn out to be the poorest. This may strike you as peculiar. Aren't these the people who have seen the light? Their initial experience of recovery has been so suddenly and overwhelmingly wonderful that they know they'll never have a problem with their old behavior again. As far as they're concerned, they're cured. Sure, they once had a problem, but now it's over. They've learned their lesson. Period.

However, no one teeters on the edge of a hard fall more than they do. Why?

Because they've allowed their experience of recovery to become rigid. Deciding that they're cured means that they've closed themselves off to further growth. Included in that growth is the usually disheartening discovery that bad feelings and rotten circumstances will continue to crop up, even in recovery. When they finally discover this, they are often not prepared. Mood swings, pain, and disappointment are somehow deeply shocking. Now that they're recovered, shouldn't they be fixed? All better? Impervious to pain?

What Twelve Step programs refer to as a "pink cloud"—the feeling of enormous well-being that some people in early recovery experience—can be wonderful. We're not suggesting that you shouldn't enjoy the new feelings of serenity, self-acceptance, connection, and the sheer relief of feeling better physically that you may feel in the early days of your recovery. But experience shows us that you have to continue to build on the structure of recovery we wrote about in the last chapter. That includes finding and depending on a support network and developing new behaviors. If you don't put sufficient energy into this, when a negative feeling does come, when the pink cloud lifts, it can come like a knockout blow. Everything may seem to topple all at once. Sometimes the only recourse you can think of is the one you know best—your old compulsive behavior.

For people who have abstained from self-destructive compulsive behaviors over a long time, it seems that the best recovery is slow recovery. You need to take it easy. Now that you don't have the buffer of alcohol, other drugs, or other behaviors that used to help you block out your feelings and pain, you have to expect to feel vulnerable.

Even if you do feel something akin to a pink cloud, this feeling of well-being is still a feeling. Like all feelings, it has built-in obsolescence. Other feelings will eventually move in, more warm fronts and low fronts, more rain and sleet, as well as more days of sunshine. Recovery seems largely a process of preparing for this inevitable emotional weather. Realize first that uncomfortable feelings will return, and second that all your feelings will pass and others will take their place.

What doesn't have to pass is your moment-to-moment resolve to stick it out, secure in the knowledge that what you're going through at any given moment isn't forever. Many recovering people say they find enormous relief in the simple truth that whatever they're going through now will pass. But how do you learn to tolerate the bad stuff when it hits? How do you prepare for the arrival of lousy emotional weather?

Those positive assumptions, that positive self-talk we suggested building up in yourself in the last chapter, is one way of constructing a strong, adaptable shelter from all this emotional weather. This shelter does, however, take time to build, and there may be moments of panic while you're building it. You may feel that your feelings are still too raw and exposed. You may begin to lose faith that you've got the fortitude to stick it out. Sometimes you can convince yourself you're lost and that the only way out is to pick up your old behavior again.

It's important to stress that even if you feel this bad, you don't *have* to go back to the old ways. Many people go down to the depths and back up again without resorting to old destructive behaviors. They draw on the sustenance of realizing that "feelings are not facts." As difficult as it may be to believe this in the depth of rage, resentment, sorrow, or depression, *you don't have to let how you feel affect how you act.* If you practice using your support network, stick to a satisfying, effective plan that gives you workable alternatives to your old behaviors, and continue to feed yourself with positive self-talk, you will have the tools to weather anything life hands you. This is not pie-in-the-sky or blind faith or a catchy little phrase of hope. Countless recovering people prove it true every day.

But in the real world sometimes people do give in. What we would like to show you now is that even if you do give in, you can make the choice to get back on track and learn how to stay on track in the future.

SLIPS, JUMPS, AND RELAPSES

The decision people sometimes make to pick up old behaviors again is more complicated than it may at first appear.

Perhaps slips and relapses sound like the same thing to you, but our definitions of the terms aren't interchangeable at all. The motivations behind what we call a slip and those behind a relapse are quite distinct. We've even come up with a third category—jumps—to describe other motivations behind the decision to pick up old behaviors again.

We're not being picky or playing with semantics in making these distinctions. We make them because we've discovered that people often have quite different motivations for picking up old behaviors again. Exploring what those motivations are can lead to a crucial preparedness. You've already learned that recovery depends on increasing your consciousness of your feelings and also of the triggers that can set you up to drink, drug, or act out in other ways.

These triggers can be subtle and insidious. You'll see just how subtle they can be as you meet the next three people, each of whom illustrates just what we mean by a slip, a jump, and a relapse. Each has learned how you can sometimes sabotage yourself by ignoring important triggers, even when you don't realize that's what you're doing. Becoming alert to this slippery self-sabotage is the task we'll explore right now.

THE ANATOMY OF A SLIP: *MICHAEL*

Michael wasn't sure he wanted to give up drinking completely. He wanted to learn how to drink "socially," but he was having a hard time with that. Not that he thought he was an alcoholic; he tended to drink only on weekends. "I guess every so often you could say I tie one on," he said, "but it's not like I drink every day. I don't drink at all during the week. I'm not stupid. I don't want to mess up my job. But, you know, the weekend comes and I want to have a good time. So I'll go out to a few bars. Nothing wrong with that, is there?"

But there did seem to be something wrong, even to Michael. Increasingly, he would end up back home or in strange apartments without having any idea of how he got there. "I know I've let things get out of hand," he said. "I guess I've been blacking out a lot. But I'm not an alcoholic. If I were a drunk, I couldn't keep off the stuff all week, could I? I just want to know how to have a normal good time on the weekends."

Michael tried limiting himself to a few beers when he went out, but it never seemed to work. "One time I even thought, okay, just go to a bar and drink club soda. I was only going there to have fun and meet people, right?" But the club soda got boring, he said. "All it made me want to do was go to the bathroom." Also, it looked too much like gin and tonic. Michael felt it was stupid to drink a drink that looked like something it wasn't. So he ordered one real drink. He ended up in another blackout.

"I guess I'd like to see if I can stay off this stuff. One of my girlfriends asked me why I didn't talk to a therapist about it or something. I'm not pigheaded. Maybe a shrink could help me cut down. So here I am."

Michael agreed to a one-week period of abstinence just to see what a complete break from alcohol might be like. By the end of the week, if things were going well and he wanted to continue, he might want to extend his abstinence by another week. He thought that sounded reasonable. He started going to an outpatient group and hooked up with a man his age, Henry, who identified himself as a recovering alcoholic but wasn't at all preachy about it. "I figure I might as well learn from the real thing," Michael said, "even if I know I don't have the same problem he does." Michael had an aversion to the label "alcoholic" and was grateful that he wasn't required to identify himself that way.

He got through his first week pretty well. At Henry's suggestions, and those of others in his therapy group, he planned a different weekend routine from his normal one. He went to a ball game with Henry, whose presence was enough to keep Michael drinking cola instead of beer. The next day he helped Henry paint his apartment. Later that night he had dinner with a group of Henry's friends. "They may not have all been recovering, Michael said, "but they didn't seem to need a drink to have a good time." Michael had a good time himself and agreed to try abstinence for another week.

Michael's next weekend, however, posed some problems. He was sick of doing so much with just Henry and thought he would spend at least one night on his own, maybe going to a movie. He was determined not to go to his usual bar. He was clear in his resolve about that. And he was relieved at the thought of being able to do something by himself. "I really felt I had this alcohol thing licked. I felt so good about just being able to be with myself." He went to a movie, bought some popcorn and soda, and tried to lose himself in the film. For some reason, however, he couldn't. He was aware of other people whispering, coughing. He couldn't get involved in the movie's plot. The air-conditioning was too strong. He felt antsy. He thought, "What the hell, nobody says I can't leave early if I want to!" So he left the movie house and decided to walk home.

It was a warm summer night. He wanted to walk through the center of town to enjoy the lights and the sight of people milling around and having a good time. But the anxiety he had felt in the movie house wouldn't leave. He passed a restaurant full of happy-looking couples. It hit him that he was alone, that he was far from having a "good time." He passed a bar, smelled the beer and booze, and heard the sound of laughter and jukebox music. It seemed to beckon to him. He was still firm in his resolve, however. He wasn't going to drink tonight, no matter what. Then he passed another bar, a quieter bar, the kind he liked going into sometimes, a place where no one would bother him. But, no, he wasn't going to go in.

"Then I thought, hey, there's no reason I can't get something to eat, is there?" He said he passed a good, cheap, brightly lit restaurant he had been to before. He even knew one of the waitresses there. He went in, glad to be in some place he knew he would be recognized. Sure enough, the waitress came over to him, smiling, greeting him warmly. "The usual?" she asked. "Sure!" Michael said. And she brought him his usual fried chicken and chips. And a pitcher of beer.

"I was going to tell her I really didn't want the beer, but something kept me from doing that. The place was so brightly lit, so friendly. It didn't look like my usual dark bar hangouts. I mean, hadn't I proven to myself I could control my drinking? I'd gone through more than a week without a drink. The beer looked so good. I knew I could handle it. So I poured myself a glass."

While Michael didn't black out that night, it was all he could do to force himself to go straight home. "I can't tell you how much I wanted to go out to my old bars," he said. "But somehow I was bent on proving to myself I could stop right then and there. God, it was torture." When Michael did get home, he tried to tell himself he was okay. "I'd gotten through a night, had something to eat, a couple beers—just like a normal person!" But he knew it wasn't really just like a normal person. Only the most desperate effort of willpower got him home without drinking more.

Michael remembered his earlier resolve not to drink, how firm he had been in it. He remembered how good he had felt the previous week and the weekend before when he had managed to have a good time without drinking. He really hadn't wanted that beer. Why did he drink it?

Henry had left a message on his answering machine to call him whenever he got in. Michael's depression deepened. He almost didn't call Henry. Then he thought, what the hell, it might not be so bad to talk to him. When he got Henry on the phone, he told him what happened. Henry listened, then asked a few questions about Michael's night up until he drank the beer. He then told Michael he had had a classic slip.

A slip is something that usually occurs in early recovery. It feels like an accident. You're going along, everything is fine, and then, as if someone other than you had arranged things, you find a drink in your hand. You're usually baffled. How did it happen? Slips seem to come out of left field. They hit you unaware.

But as Henry was able to point out to Michael, not all slips are accidental. You set yourself up for a slip in some very definite ways. Henry showed Michael that his slip began way before he got to the restaurant. His initial decision not to connect with someone for support was the first danger sign. The feeling of relief he had about being able to spend the night alone was another danger sign. Michael unconsciously felt relief because he cleared his night of any obstacles to picking up a drink. "It's not that you can't be alone," Henry said, "it's just that if you want to keep from drinking, you better have a damned good plan for yourself when you are alone." As Henry questioned him, Michael admitted that he picked the movie not because he really wanted to see it, but because it was downtown, close to the action. Michael began to realize that he had decided to walk home the way he had so he would pass a few bars. He also conveniently chose to forget that what he really liked about his usual restaurant wasn't especially how friendly the waitress was, or how good the fried chicken was, but the fact that you could get a pitcher of beer with it.

Michael conveniently forgot a lot of things. He set himself up to drink again in some definite ways. But learning that he was responsible for setting things up for himself wasn't, Henry reassured him, an invitation to beat himself up. He wasn't a bad person because he'd engineered his night the way he did. He was just a person who very much wanted to drink. And if he wanted to remain abstinent, he would have to wake up to the ways this strong and sometimes less than conscious desire to drink made him work against himself.

Slips feel like they slip in without your awareness, without your conscious desire for them. But when you look at what leads up to a slip, you always find that in some way you've cleared the way for it. Maintaining a network of support and sticking to a plan of healthy alternatives will alert you to behaviors that may lead to a slip.

THE ANATOMY OF A JUMP:
LENA

Lena was a striking woman in her early twenties—slight, with blue-black hair, very fair skin, and bright, wide, dark eyes. She had been an avid club-goer and self-professed groupie of several underground rock bands. "I never felt really alive unless there was some kind of danger around me. It just wasn't fun any other way." Danger to her meant hanging out at clubs until the early morning, meeting strange guys, sometimes going to bed with them, and often doing drugs with them until they were all so wasted that they crashed at whoever's place was nearest.

But Lena had made an attempt to cool it. "I got so tired of all that stuff, of all the brainless jerks I kept getting stuck with. And of feeling like garbage the next day. It's not like I want to become a health freak or anything. I don't want to turn into Mother Teresa either. I just want to cool off. Figure out how to live in daylight."

Lena couldn't figure out how to do that. "How do people get up and go to work and come home and watch the evening news and eat dinner and go to bed at a reasonable hour? How do normal people get normal?" Lena had a job as a secretary at a publishing company that did art books. She felt she was hired as much for her looks as for any skills she had. She had been able to get away with coming in late in the afternoon and working into the early evenings because the editor she worked for kept similar hours and led a similar lifestyle. But that editor had just gotten fired, and Lena was transferred to someone else, someone who actually slept at night and got to work by 9:30 in the morning. "At first I was going to quit," she said. "But then I thought, maybe this is what I need, someone normal to work with. Maybe I can get out of the boring rut my life is in."

Lena was sick enough of drugs that she somehow forced herself to quit, cold turkey. She even started going to NA meetings. "I'd always known where they were. My club friends were in and out of NA all the time. Some meetings had gotten positively trendy. If you weren't at a club, you were probably at an NA meeting. I thought, hell, I can cleanse my soul with the best of 'em. I went to Sunday school as a kid, didn't I?"

But Lena quickly grew bored with NA. She couldn't get the Steps. The only thing she was sure of was she was depressed. And while she was sick of what drugs did to her, nothing else seemed to be much better. She had done pills mostly—ups at night, downs to get her to sleep for a few hours, ups to get going again. "Classic Judy Garland," she said. "I was a chemical schizo." She had managed to stay clean for a few weeks, but she was feeling real wavery. Her new, normal schedule made her feel like a martian. She wasn't sure how long she could hold out. At her lowest moments, suicide didn't seem at all out of the question.

So she decided to try an outpatient clinic. Although she was perfectly willing to call herself a drug addict, she admitted to being grateful to be around other people who didn't instantly identify themselves as addicts. "I guess I was put off by that in NA. It's like I was sick of defining myself just as an addict. I mean, I am a human being too, I think. Anyway, I'm trying to be a human being." She began to warm up to the group after a while. Her hard street-smart exterior began to soften a bit. Once she even cried as she described the despair of a typical 4:00 A.M. debauch, and the terrible emptiness she felt all day afterwards. She was softening, letting other people in a bit more. She even looked a little different—less brittle, less aggressively punk.

But she had a hard time taking her new, good feelings about herself out of the group and into the rest of her life. It was foreign for her to pick up the phone to ask for help at the worst times, despite repeated encouragement from other group members. Lena seemed able to accept support only in group therapy; outside that room she said she felt like an animal in a jungle. She was closed, wary, ready to pounce or flee. "That's how the real world is," she said. "If I walked around like I was in group therapy all the time, I'd be dead." Her despair wasn't getting much better. And though she tried to be as responsive as she could to the demands of her new, conservative boss, one day she lost it.

"I screwed up with a phone message," she said. "Someone important called and I didn't write it down like I usually do on one of those pink 'While You Were Out' slips. I scribbled it on a scrap of paper, which must have fallen into the trash or something. I had a pile of things to do that afternoon and I just forgot. Well, this real important guy—some president or something—called back a couple hours later yelling that how dare my boss not return his important call and leave him hanging about this extremely important deal.

"I don't know, something just snapped. I told this guy he was a pompous windbag who I wouldn't give the time of day to, and if he couldn't start talking to me like a human being I'd hang up on him right then and there. Actually, he hung up on me. He got through on some other line to my boss, who then called me in to fire me."

Lena said she was almost glad. "I was sick up to here with this stupid normal job I was trying to keep. Maybe I was a martian. Maybe I just wasn't cut out for human life. To hell with all of it. I felt an inordinate need to get zonked. For a brief moment, I thought of calling someone in my group. But no, I was pissed at everybody—even all those 'nice' people who offered me support. Besides, anybody who had a day like mine deserved a real break." She made a beeline for her old dealer and stocked up on a nice big cocktail of barbiturates. She sat back and waited for the familiar oblivion.

"Hey," she said in group. "What's the big deal? I used to get high all the time. Now I get high one time under completely forgivable circumstances. I didn't even enjoy it that much, and you guys are on my case."

You Know When You're About to Jump

Lena leaped. What happened to her wasn't a slip. It was an out-and-out jump.

What is a jump? A jump is different from a slip because you're fully aware you're doing it. You don't feel remorseful when you jump. You feel defiant.

Not all jumps are as overtly self-destructive as Lena's. Sometimes you jump simply when you decide you're going to prove that you can be a "moderate" user. People who have never before been able to control their drinking, other drug use, or other self-destructive behavior jump when they decide that this time is going to be different. Lena was only really conscious that she wanted to escape. "I never really accepted that I couldn't go back to drugs, make them somehow work for me. I realize now I was just waiting for the trigger to get my rage going. I had so much anger buried in me. I was like gas waiting for a match."

Lena realized she never really allowed herself to recover because she kept holding onto the deeply held belief that she could stop being an addict but still be a controlled user. "Drugs couldn't be an everyday thing, but surely they could be a once-in-awhile option." Like Michael, she set herself up by putting herself in extremely uncomfortable circumstances without having enough support to deal with them.

But now, she says, "I've begun to realize I can get help—give myself help—even when I'm out of a therapist's office. I can call people during the day. I can even go to a meeting at lunch time." An NA meeting? "Yeah. Now that I've decided I really do want help, I don't think they're so jerky anymore."

Letting down your guard, truly letting help in, can bring astonishing relief. "It's as if something in me was so tight and coiled up; I was an explosion waiting to happen," Lena says. "Somehow, I've allowed that tension to let go a little. And I accept that I can't do this alone. Slowly, I'm starting to feel better about myself. More hopeful. It's not that I think I can turn into Suzy Homemaker or even a normal nine-to-five secretary. But I don't have to kill myself to get what I want. I'm sure of that now. There's an easier way. This support-and-plan business really does work if you let it. I'm starting to accept that maybe I'm not a martian, maybe I really am a human being."

The Angry Jump

Anger often fuels jumps. You're not alone if you discover that there seems to be an endless pool of rage inside you. People preparing to jump often give themselves the following angry message: "What's the use? I'm not like other people. I'm just not cut out for recovery. Anyway, who says I can't do whatever I want to? I can control my behavior. I really wasn't that bad. Can't I have a good time if I want to? I'm not some baby." Prospective jumpers can work themselves up to quite a zealous pitch. Defiance defines them. So, it often turns out, does denial.

Just as people who slip ignore the triggers that cause them to slip, people who jump conveniently forget that they never were able to control their behavior before. You may be headed for a jump when your anger or self-righteousness begins to consume you, when you start to feel defiant about everyone and everything in your life. It's a warning sign, anyway. But, like Lena, you may find that your anger and defiance are fueled by something deeper—fear. There's a fear that what other recovering people are telling you might actually be true. They keep saying that if you let your guard down and open up a bit, something like help—even love—might get through.

Unlike a jump or a slip, which usually happens in early sobriety, a relapse can happen years into recovery—with devastating effect. It's the third and most difficult of the reversions recovering people sometimes make. The hard truth is that a lot of people who have true relapses don't make it back to recovery. But that doesn't mean they can't come back. As you'll discover in this story, you can come back even when your despair and your relapse are as severe as Tom's.

BACK FROM THE DEPTHS OF A RELAPSE: *TOM*

Tom felt he had made a lot of progress, and he had. He was once an active heroin addict and alcoholic, labels he freely applied to himself. "Under the influence," there didn't seem much else in which he didn't compulsively overindulge. Sex, food, stealing when he didn't have money, overspending when he did—he said it was like the whole world was made only to give him stuff to get high on. "I thought people were around only to supply me with money, drugs, booze, and sex. Nothing else mattered."

Despite his overindulgence in whatever he could get his hands on, Tom somehow managed to keep up enough of a "normal" front to hold down jobs in construction or carpentry. A big, strong, beefy guy, he was a good worker when he wasn't too out of it. "Sometimes I made pretty good money, which meant I could get wasted for days at a time," he said.

Tom hit what he called his bottom when he got into a fight in a bar with three other guys and ended up in the hospital. "They beat the crap out of me," he said. It wasn't so much the severity of the beating that got to him—he had been beaten up plenty of times. What got to him was the time he had to himself in his hospital bed. Tom had what you might think of as the classic recovery experience. "I understood right off what Twelve Step programs mean when they talk about spiritual awakenings," Tom says. "That's what I had in the hospital. Not because I was in a hospital—that had happened enough times before. I'd been in jail a number of times too. I had no illusions that the stuff I was doing to myself was messing me up. I just never cared before. I never cared that I was killing myself.

"But somehow this time I started to care. I was all stitched up. I felt lousy. But something inside moved in me. For the first time in my life, I didn't want to continue doing what I'd always done. I really wanted to get out of the mess my life had become. I don't know how to put it into words. It was just this strong, warm, comforting knowledge. Somehow I wanted to change— and I knew I could. It really did hit me in a flash."

We haven't talked much about spiritual awakenings, an idea that intimidates a lot of prospective recovering people because of its "God" sound. But this book has been about awakenings from the very first page. Greg, the person in this book's first story, awakened to the fact that he was afraid of being out of control and was able to acknowledge it. He wouldn't have called this awakening "spiritual," and you don't have to either. But sometimes the force of an awakening can be very strong, particularly when it reveals the fact that you truly want to change your behavior and your life. And sometimes it feels natural to call it spiritual because it seems to come from somewhere outside you, some source of strength larger than yourself.

"I really did surrender," Tom said. "That's the only word for it. And I wasn't the type of guy who admitted to something like that easily. I was a junkie, a drunk, and I'd just tried to beat up three guys bigger than me. Up until that moment, I was hell-bent on proving that I could make the world do what I wanted it to. But suddenly, that day in the hospital, I just let all that go. I wanted things to be different. I realized that I actually wanted and needed help."

Tom knew about AA. After one stint in jail, as a condition of his release, he had to go to a month of meetings. "I had to get the chairman of each meeting to sign this affidavit. It was a real drag," he said. Going to those meetings had no effect back then, but at least it taught him where some meetings were now that he wanted to go to one.

Tom didn't resist any of the suggestions he received in AA. He got a sponsor. He started working the Steps. He made new recovering friends. He read the literature. And slowly, just as they told him it would, his life got better. A lot better.

He started getting more and more lucrative jobs. After a year and a half of sobriety, he decided to start his own contracting business. Now that people could depend on him to show up, his business grew. His skills improved. He began making more money. He had lived in a series of flophouses before he started recovery; now he was renting a small house with a workroom in the garage. He bought a truck. He went to meetings, began chairing some of them, making coffee at others. Two years into his sobriety, he met a woman with whom he fell in love. They began talking about marriage.

People who knew Tom at this time glowed when they spoke of him. "I've never seen such a transformation." ... "God, you should have heard him talk at yesterday's meeting. I've never been so moved." Tom was having a wonderful recovery, everyone agreed. Tom did too. "I can't believe how good my life has gotten," he said. "God willing, I'll never pick up another drink or drug in my life."

Then, after nearly three years of sobriety, came what Tom now refers to as Black November. In rapid succession, the following happened:

- A fire broke out in Tom's house and workroom, destroying most of his tools. Because Tom didn't have insurance, he was ruined, bankrupt.
- The woman he was seeing suddenly announced she didn't love him anymore. In fact, she had been seeing another man for some time behind Tom's back, a guy Tom had regarded as one of his best friends.
- Tom's sponsor had a heart attack and died.

One of Tom's cronies from his drinking and drugging days happened to come back into town after all this happened and looked him up. He had no idea Tom hadn't had a drink or a drug in nearly three years. After reminiscing with Tom about the "good times," he said, "Let's go out for a few brews." Tom remembers this moment vividly, like it all happened in slow motion.

"It's like what they say happens the moment before you die," he said. "In a moment, my whole life—before and during sobriety—flashed in front of me. I was crystal-clear about it. The whole thing had been a fraud, a waste. All the slogans and recovery stuff I learned seemed like playroom stuff and a bunch of nonsense. I looked at my old drinking buddy and said, 'Sure, let's go.'" Tom said his return to drinking was as cold-blooded as it could have been. "Nothing mattered anymore. I made a completely conscious choice. At least that's what it felt like then."

Tom quickly returned to his old pattern of drinking and drugging. His life completely collapsed. He stayed out of recovery, quickly becoming homeless, a "bum" for two years.

And then one morning in a men's shelter it happened again. He had had enough. "It was agony to go back to a meeting," he said. "But, hell, my whole life had been agony. I was beaten again. But somehow there was still a flame inside me. Something in me still wanted to live. So I came crawling back. And now, one day at a time, I'm learning to cope with life again. I also know I'm one of the lucky ones. A lot of guys who go through the kind of stuff I went through never come back. A lot of those guys are dead, I know. I watched them die on the street in knife fights, from strokes, from hypothermia when they passed out in a snowbank. I don't know why I've hung on. I don't know where the hell this new hope I feel comes from. I only know I've got it. And it feels stronger now than it ever felt before."

Again, Tom's story may strike you as stereotypical, perhaps the kind of story you expected from this book. A nice guy hit hard by life whose drinking and drugging left him homeless and on the streets. But what happened to him internally—the shock of dealing with some terrible blows, circumstances that seemed to be worse *after* he started to recover than they had ever been before—may sound like your story. You don't have to hit skid row to understand the emotional devastation Tom went through. And the real lesson here has to do with understanding the nature of the relapse he had.

Relapses are very different from slips and jumps. A true relapse happens not because of motivational problems or a lack of basic sobriety skills. It happens when your coping mechanisms are overwhelmed and your emotional resources are depleted. Often, tragic circumstances precede it—a friend dies, you lose your job, your lover leaves you. Something causes you intense suffering and despair. Sometimes you are suddenly faced with seemingly unresolvable conflicts. Or ugly memories rise unexpectedly, seemingly from nowhere, taking you by surprise and leaving you with feelings of guilt, shame, or other feelings you have a hard time dealing with.

Tom was able to come back from his relapse with even greater resolve to "live rather than die." And he gained insights about needing to develop his faith. Although some people never come back from a relapse, many do finally come to grips with issues they needed to resolve to continue recovery. With courage, even a terrible experience like a full-blown relapse can be an opportunity to learn about yourself.

It may seem as if we've traveled far away from Step Zero territory. Here we're talking about what can happen two or three years down the line, and you may still be deciding whether or not you even want to change your behavior, and your life.

But we're really still where you are. All we've done is map out the large territory of possibilities. We hope this map has offered you a wider perspective, one that you may want to use to evaluate your own behavior and the effect it may be having on your life. We're not telling you to do anything or suggesting that you choose one program or action over another. We're not urging you to recover in any one way. All we have hoped to do is to help you take a new look at some of the things recovery might mean if you decided to give it a try.

What we're really talking about is opening up your thinking to the possibility that living consciously may give you more fulfillment and hope. Achieving that consciousness, as you've seen throughout this book, doesn't require buying any particular recovery line or labeling yourself an addict. Increasing your consciousness depends on your attitude. It's an attitude that allows you to see life as an adventure with any number of unanticipated hills and valleys, but one richly worth taking.

You can choose whatever vehicle you would like to ride through this adventure—Twelve Step programs, outpatient clinics, the support of friends and family, one-on-one therapy, or a combination of these. That's all up to you. Of course, if one vehicle doesn't feel right, you can always get off and try another.

Our experience has proven to us again and again how wonderful the journey can be. We hope that you've found abundant reason in these pages to believe that this journey is worth taking, and that *you* can take it.

CHAPTER EIGHT

Ten Questions and Answers About Recovery

As much as you may have developed a new perspective about addiction and recovery, you've undoubtedly still got some specific questions that we haven't addressed yet. We don't expect to second-guess all of those questions here, but perhaps we can anticipate some of the more basic ones.

The following ten questions have grown out of our experience with thousands of recovering and prospective recovering people. As you'll see, there are rarely any easy or black-and-white answers to questions about recovery. But there are always more productive ways to start grappling with them than you may at first realize.

Question #1 *How do I know if I'm really addicted?*

The most sensible definition of "addiction" we can come up with runs something like this: If you've found it impossible to quit any behavior that is significantly impairing your life—whether in external ways or in the way you feel about yourself—you're a candidate for the kind of recovery we've been talking about in this book.

Notice we didn't say you were an addict. Some people benefit from identifying themselves as addicts because it answers what seems to be a basic question about themselves in a simple way. But other people do not feel this way; they may feel limited or intimidated by the term. What you call yourself doesn't matter. What matters is coming to a decision about whether or not you need help with a behavior that has proven to be self-destructive and that you can't control.

You may be wondering something else: Is there a difference between abusing alcohol or drugs and being addicted to them?

There is an important distinction to be made between abuse and addiction. Abusers may push their use of a certain substance or behavior to where it interferes with their lives. But when they are finally convinced that the consequences of their behavior are really hurtful, they are able to see the logic of stopping and are able to stop. Those who struggle with addiction usually continue no matter what the consequences. The behavior is just too compelling to stop, even if they clearly see it as self-destructive. In other words, if you're struggling with addiction, you're struggling with behavior that's out of control and not responsive to any rational decision you may try to make to stop it. If you know you're not going to get pleasure from something but you do it anyway, you're a definite candidate for recovery.

Question #2 *Let's say I manage to give up cocaine. Does that mean I can't drink? Do I have to give up everything?*

It's true that you can be hooked to cocaine and not have exactly the same addictive response to alcohol. Or you can be an alcoholic but not necessarily have the same addictive response to something else. In general, though, we suggest total abstinence for people attempting to recover from any one substance or behavior. Why?

For several reasons. First, many people eventually discover that any drug or behavior—even if it's not their primary choice and they have no history of being hooked to it—can trigger the desire for the drug or behavior that *is* their primary choice. This is especially true of people who have ceased cocaine use but still drink. They often find that alcohol gets rid of their inhibitions enough to trigger a return to cocaine. In other words, indulging in a mood-altering but allegedly less dangerous behavior too often makes you vulnerable to eventually indulging in the behavior you know to be more dangerous—the one you want to give up.

But there's another more basic reason why we suggest total abstinence. The whole point of recovery is to learn nonchemical and nonaddictive ways to cope with life. For example, if you drink instead of doing cocaine, alcohol may leave you as ill-equipped to cope with life as you were when you did cocaine. There are also some practical social reasons why total abstinence works best in recovery. If you hook up with a Twelve Step program or another group, you'll quickly feel out of step with everyone else who is practicing total abstinence. You might be saying, "Who the hell cares what they think?" But since support is so important to maintaining abstinence from the substance or behavior you want to give up, why jeopardize that support by being an outsider when you don't have to?

We're talking primarily about alcohol and other drugs here. Food, sex, work, and money addictions sometimes require a slightly different perspective, as do addictions to nicotine and caffeine. It may seem a little odd to the newcomer to see so many recovering alcoholics smoking cigarettes and drinking coffee. Haven't they just substituted one addiction for another? Remember, however, the wisdom Suzanne discovered back in

Chapter Six when she quoted a friend who advised her to "deal with your addictions in the order in which they'll kill you." All addictive behavior may be seen as destructive, but for people who identify themselves as alcoholic, alcohol has proven to be infinitely more dangerous to them than nicotine or caffeine. Smoking and drinking coffee are far preferable to the complete, devastating ruin they know that alcohol would bring.

One of the most important slogans to remember in recovery is "progress, not perfection." Sometimes you have to let up on yourself and accept the fact that while you may not be able to give up everything all at once, you have every reason to celebrate the fact that you've given up the addiction that threatens you the most. The rest, given time, will more than likely lift if you continue to practice the principles of recovery you've begun to learn about.

Question #3 *If I decide I do have a problem with alcohol or other drugs, is it dangerous for me to take any medication, even if my doctor prescribes it?*

When a medication is prescribed for a bona fide medical condition, and as long as it's not addictive or mood-altering, unlike sleeping pills, tranquilizers, stimulants, or narcotic pain-killers, we would certainly advise you to take it. Just be honest with yourself and with your doctor. Let him or her know that you're concerned about the addictive properties of drugs that may be prescribed. Even more important, choose your doctors on the basis of whether they have experience working with people struggling with addictions. There are still a lot of "Dr. Feelgoods" out there only too willing to prescribe anything you want. Be alert and steer clear of doctors who tell you it "doesn't matter" if you take a moderate dose of barbiturates. If you're struggling with addiction, it can matter a lot.

Question #4 *I've decided I may be an alcoholic. Can I go to any Twelve Step meeting that's available, even if it's not AA? Would any of the others work as well?*

It's a good idea in early recovery to develop close contact with people who share your particular addictive problem, sometimes for very practical reasons. The cocaine addict, for example, typically experiences horrendous, urgent, physical cravings that are often very different from many alcoholics' sometimes more low-grade desires to drink. A cocaine addict surrounded by alcoholics in early recovery just won't feel quite the same complete identification he may need to feel to get as much as possible out of the group. Similarly, an alcoholic usually benefits most, at least in early recovery, from hearing how other alcoholics are doing. The same with overeaters, sexually compulsive people, or people who compulsively spend money. One thing we can say just about categorically is that going through a general group therapy that doesn't offer help specifically for your addictive behavior will almost certainly be a waste of time. You need to be around people who have dealt with the problem you're dealing with, at least at the beginning of recovery.

This said, there can be something wonderfully healing in making connections with people who are struggling with different addictive behaviors from your own. Once you've managed to survive the hurdles of dealing with your particular problem in early recovery, you generally find that issues of self-esteem, building a bridge back to a nonaddictive lifestyle, and learning new coping skills are similar for any recovering person. Listening to people struggling with other problems can be revelatory in another way too. When you begin to recover in any one area, there's often a domino effect—you may begin to identify other areas of your life that will benefit from being treated as "addictions."

We've seen so many people in group therapy blossom as they come in contact with other people—even if their addictions are different. The feeling of "being in this together" can be wonderfully healing. Given the proliferation of people who are addicted to more than one substance and behavior, and the proliferation of groups that have been formed to help them, it seems foolish not to take advantage of the broad range of help now abundantly available.

Question #5 *I've always heard that marijuana isn't addictive. Is this true?*

After alcohol, marijuana is the most widely used drug in the United States. It far outstrips even cocaine, and it's certainly ahead of heroin, crack, and other drugs. But is it addictive?

Yes. Absolutely.

What seems to keep many people from accepting that marijuana is addictive comes from two things: (1) the long time it often takes before obvious damage from using the drug can be seen, and (2) pot's relatively positive public image.

First, the time problem. As is often the case with alcohol, it can take years before any damage resulting from marijuana use is evident, and even then the cause of the damage may still not appear to be pot. Because marijuana tends to sap ambition, make you less focused, decrease cognitive function, and increase feelings of passivity and apathy—all usually over a long period of time—you may only be able to identify the problem as something like chronic depression or listlessness. And if you decide to seek help, it's often psychiatric or other therapeutic treatment that never gets to the root of the problem: you've been smoking marijuana for years!

Then there's the public image reason. The relatively good press that marijuana received in the 1960s and 1970s created perceptions about it that largely continue to this day. Isn't pot natural, a gentle consciousness-raiser, a symbol of free love, peace? What could be wrong with that?

The hard truth is that marijuana has impaired the lives of thousands of people. Just because it may not produce the kind of decline or signs of dependency of other drugs doesn't mean it can't lead to the same kind of devastation. And, of course, it's a common trigger drug. Marijuana often leads to other drug use or behaviors that threaten you more dramatically.

Question #6 *Why do some people have problems with addictive behavior while others don't? In other words, why me?*

First of all, the jury is still out about whether certain addictions are the result of nature or nurture—that is, are they genetically inherited or learned? Certainly, if you come from a family that has produced numerous alcoholics, you would be well advised to be on the alert for its reappearance in you. But what may be the genetic causes of addiction and what may be other causes are rarely easy—in fact, usually impossible—to detect.

The clearest reason that some people seem to have more problems with addiction than others can be expressed with the following analogy. Think of addiction as a fuel that needs a spark to burn. The fuel is what's inside you—usually a high level of stress, perhaps combined with a genetic susceptibility to reacting in certain ways to certain substances; a combination of psychological and physical stuff that seeks urgent release. When this fuel builds up enough, it doesn't take much to set it off. It's ready for the spark. You may provide that spark when you take a drink, do other drugs, eat, have sex, spend money, or go to work. If your fuel level is high enough, one or another action may easily turn into a spark and ignite it. Addiction is often the result.

Certain people, for whatever reason, seem to have persistently high fuel levels. They have to be careful, therefore, when they come into contact with any potential spark. Combustion, or the addiction, is always waiting to happen. To continue the analogy, recovery from addiction means doing two things: (1) attempting to reduce your fuel levels as much as possible, and (2) avoiding sparks.

Why high fuel levels seem to occur in some people more than others ends up not being terribly important. The fact is, it is a problem for some people and those people are well advised to deal with it. We've never met a diabetic who wanted to be diabetic, but we've never met one who wanted to get better who didn't take steps to keep his or her illness under control. That's what this recovery is about too. Concentrating on the solutions we've been exploring in this book always seems more profitable than worrying about causes that nobody fully understands.

Question #7 *I've decided to seek a therapist to help me with recovery. Is it best to find one who's in recovery too?*

It's been our experience that this is one of the least important variables in choosing a therapist. In fact, a therapist's credentials are largely irrelevant, but a therapist's experience working successfully with addiction is absolutely relevant. You should certainly find out about that experience. It's important to choose a therapist who specializes in or at least frequently works with people struggling with addictive behaviors.

What's perhaps most important is how you feel going to your therapist. Any treatment professional who threatens that "you'll probably use again if you don't do it my way" is, from our perspective, a poor therapist. We've seen too many coerced recovering people simply give up when they found they couldn't do it somebody else's way. As we've said, statistics make it very clear that no one method of treating addiction has a greater success rate than any other. What seems to matter are the motivation and attitudes, not only of the recovering person, but of the therapist.

A therapist who will help you is a therapist who not only has experience treating addiction, but who makes you feel comfortable. This is the crucial question to ask: Is it helping? If, after giving a therapist a fair try, you discover it's not helping you, then you have every right to choose someone else.

We realize that this is often far easier said than done. In the raw and vulnerable state many newly recovering people are in, it may be tempting to believe a therapist who says you don't know anything. You may even think that your resentment and resistance in therapy are signs that you need to be there. But if that resentment and resistance never let up, if you realize that you simply don't like or aren't getting anything from what your therapist is telling you, you're with the wrong therapist.

Just as we believe you have the capacity to decide to recover, we believe you have the capacity to decide what the best means are to accomplish that recovery. Remain open, give various options a fair try, and then choose.

Question #8 *Do I have to tell my family or involve them in my recovery?*

It depends on your relationship with your family. Some people benefit enormously by making their family a part of their recovery. For one thing, family members are often so relieved by the usually dramatic changes for the better in the recovering addict that they quite spontaneously want to offer support. They're eager for the chance to reinforce the decision to quit that the recovering person has made.

But many family relationships are not so supportive, even if they may appear to be outwardly. Our ties to family are usually emotionally charged, and it's likely a good idea to develop a firm outside support system that you can depend on no matter what your family's response to your recovery turns out to be.

There's also the truth that as much as family members may have disliked the recovering person's behavior when he or she was acting out, they grew to depend on certain dynamics that prevailed. And they may miss those dynamics, even if rationally they know they were destructive. One husband, for example, began to resent all the time his recovering wife spent with new recovering friends. He no longer felt as needed as when he continually had to bail her out of difficulty because of her drinking and drugging. Al-Anon may be a good recovery and support alternative to suggest to your family. Equivalents to Al-Anon exist for other addictions besides alcohol—Nar-Anon, for example. Addictive behavior affects everyone in your life. It is, in fact, a family disease, and loved ones can benefit enormously by addressing what may have become their own "disease" of adapting to your addictive behavior.

Of course, if you come from a family of alcoholics or other drug addicts, none of whom are in recovery themselves, it's rarely a good idea to try to involve them in your recovery. And it's often dangerous to try to get them into recovery, especially when you're just starting out. Some good advice you'll hear a lot in Twelve Step meetings is, Keep the focus on yourself. You can't do anything for anyone else until you've helped yourself. And because recovery is such a slow process, it's usually wise to put a good deal of time and energy into your own recovery before you even attempt to help another family member. In other words, stay away from anything that threatens your recovery, even if it's your family.

Question #9 *People keep telling me if I don't go into an inpatient rehab, I'll just pick up again. Do inpatient rehabs have a better success rate than outpatient rehabs or just going to Twelve Step meetings?*

From the evidence available to us, no. Studies that have compared the results of all methods of addiction therapy indicate that there is no significant statistical difference among success rates of inpatient and outpatient rehabs or solely attending Twelve Step meetings. Success was defined as abstaining from alcohol and other drugs over a long time.

But deciding whether or not to participate, for example, in an inpatient or an outpatient rehabilitation facility shouldn't be arbitrary. Some people at the beginning of recovery respond positively to the kind of total environment approach offered in inpatient treatment facilities.

We tend to favor outpatient treatment to inpatient treatment. Outpatient therapy allows you to continue your connection to the real world. It's often a big shock to someone who's been in an inpatient rehab to reenter the world. We tend to feel that the more you can work on your addictive problems in the context of your real life, the better the lessons you learn will stick, and the less your recovery will be jeopardized when something throws you for a loop. As you've seen from some of the stories in this book, many recovering people just don't want the stigma of having been "put away." And many simply feel threatened by the thought of being taken completely out of their regular lives. Being able to return to the safety of something familiar—home, job, relationships—is essential to their feeling of well-being.

But, again, your own instincts have to be your guide. Remember that recovery only has a chance of sticking when you do it for yourself. Once the desire to recover has been awakened in you, it's important to choose whatever recovery option will continue to address and satisfy that desire. Let your mind and heart lead you to the one you think will work best for you.

Question #10 *Can I stop on my own?*

A study of heroin addicts who managed to maintain abstinence over a long time—without any outside help such as Twelve Step programs or inpatient or outpatient treatment—does seem to indicate that you can, under certain circumstances, stop an addictive behavior on your own.

But those "certain circumstances" end up being significant. The study found that while these heroin addicts did not make use of a Twelve Step program, inpatient or outpatient treatment, or any other source of addiction therapy, they all developed some kind of support system that they regularly depended on. What this means is that after making the decision to stop using heroin, they stayed away from their drug dealers, ceased contact with fellow drug users, and otherwise changed their environment and the people in it in significant ways. They built new lives for themselves. They turned to people who weren't involved in their former drug world, who reinforced the decision they made not to do heroin. They created for themselves exactly the kind of support and action plan we've identified in this book as crucial components for an effective and lasting recovery.

We are, of course, biased. We see people who are seeking help. And we've created our outpatient institute because we believe so strongly that help can be offered to anyone who wants to overcome habitual, self-destructive behavior. But the main point is, you don't have to reinvent the wheel. If sources of help exist, why not make use of them? While there have been a few addicts and alcoholics who seem to have been able to stop on their own, it is extremely difficult to do it solo. And since the benefits of participating in the kind of recovery we've been describing go far beyond simply learning not to drink, use other drugs, or act out, but include teaching you new, rewarding coping skills that end up making your whole life better, why not take advantage of it?

As with nearly every question about recovery, there are no black-and-white answers about the right or wrong way to quit. But there is an increasingly abundant store of wisdom available about different methods and perspectives you can make use of if you decide you want to quit. It's true that not everyone responds equally well to the approach offered by Twelve Step programs and certain other therapeutic alternatives. But one-on-one therapy can be effective, as can hooking up with one or two other recovering people you might meet in a group whose friendship and support you feel comfortable with.

The bottom line is, if you're hungry for recovery a lot of nourishment already exists to serve you. Why not take advantage of it? You'll know when you've found what's right for you.

Index

Other titles that will interest you...

Step Zero   *Audio Cassette*
Getting to Recovery
   featuring Arnold M. Washton, Ph.D.,
   and Nannette Stone-Washton
   A dynamic adaptation of the book, *Step Zero: Getting to Recovery*, this 90-minute audio cassette deals directly and honestly with the common concerns of someone not yet ready to take Step One. Washton and Stone-Washton offer practical help in overcoming the fear of change, letting go of negative assumptions, building a new vision, and handling relapse.
Order No. 5648

The Addictive Personality
Roots, Rituals, and Recovery
   by Craig Nakken, C.C.D.P., M.S.W.
   Why do people become addicted? What role does society play in the addiction process? This intriguing book answers these questions and looks at the common denominators of addiction. Craig Nakken will help you better understand your own, or a loved one's, chemical dependency or compulsive behavior. 12 pp.
Order No. 5149
